EASY GARDENING

EASY GARDENING

A PRACTICAL AND INSPIRATIONAL GUIDE

NANCY GARDINER

Dedicated with grateful thanks to all the people who have
so generously shared their gardens and flowers with me through
the years, without whom this book would not have been possible.

Foreword

Gardening is one of life's deep and rewarding pleasures. Once you have taken that first step of putting a plant in the ground, you will surely never be the same again, for becoming a gardener means that every day brings some new experience. It may be a sense of awe and wonder that a tiny seed, brown and dull, the size of a pinhead, can grow into a plant with roots going deep down into the nurturing soil and stems and leaves reaching out to the sun. Or perhaps just a feeling of utter joy at the sight of a newly unfurled leaf, of a fragile blossom braving a cold spring day, or a mighty tree, bereft of leaves, showing its majestic structure. Or a deep gratitude for the chance to observe and appreciate on an early morning walk, when spider webs are spangled with dew, to welcome into the new day a slowly opening rose.

People meeting for the first time in a garden become friends for life, and seeds and plants lovingly given become living reminders of that friendship.

Gardening pleasure is like no other pleasure in the world. It is ongoing, with a never-ending wish to learn more about the soil, of seeking advice from others. Get to know but never take for granted the extraordinary power of our good earth as it brings plants to life and to fruition. Revel in a sense of achievement as your tender care helps produce the first flowers or fruit. If there are frustrations, each one will bring with it new knowledge, new wisdom to help you care for the plants in your garden. And even the fatigue at the end of a day's digging and planting will just add to the warm feeling of fulfilment.

Gardening is a worthwhile and gratifying undertaking. Enjoy every minute of it!

Nancy Gardiner

June 2002

Contents

Specifics & solutions

Care & maintenance

Laying the ground-work

This section outlines the ground-work needed for a beautiful and manageable garden. A garden that will meet the needs of your family for relaxation, entertainment and privacy. Whether you are starting a new garden or renovating an old one, there are questions to be answered on planning and other basic considerations before planting can take place.

Two tall and slender conifers extend an invitation to take the path through the garden and on to the house which has been painted in typical Provençal terracotta and blue. These colours are repeated in the containers of terracotta and splashes of blue in the beds. The abundance of green in the planting brings a quiet serenity to the garden.

Site & design

At the very beginning, analyse your site – and your needs. What do you have? What size, what slope, what aspect? In what state is your garden? What do you want out of it? What functions, what fun, what style?

A new garden

Have you just moved into a new house? Is there a sea of mud or dust, with odd bits of concrete lying about, and not a green leaf to be seen anywhere? Don't despair! This is your home, your refuge, your own private place. And now you want to make a garden, as an extension of the house, a place where you can express yourself, find peace and quiet and share nature's beauty with family and friends.

To avoid spoiling your beautiful new carpets you will need to make a mud-free or dust-free access to the house, which can be done very easily with the use of purpose-made stepping stones, bricks or even planks. These, together with a sturdy welcome mat and foot scraper will save a lot of heartache. Then make sure that all those chunks of concrete, broken bricks and pieces of cement bag are cleared away and removed.

You may need to spray weed killer on to large areas infested with perennial weeds, but do this with great care. Once these basic chores are done, you will feel much better and will be able to give plenty of thought to the new garden which is to take shape and bring you many years of pleasure.

FUNCTIONS

Think about your family, your lifestyle. These will determine what you want out of your garden. Do you have small children needing a safe, shaded play area? Do you love outdoor entertaining involving a patio, built-in barbecue, boma, jacuzzi? Is a formal, 'adult' garden with tranquil water features your ideal?

What about a swimming-pool? Do you dream of a vegetable, fruit and herb garden? A greenhouse for orchids or a potting shed? Will the entrance to your property display your house and much of the garden – or are seclusion and privacy paramount? Do you want to attract wildlife to your garden? Where will you place one or more convenient utility areas for wash lines, rubbish bins, garden shed, storing a boat, and so on?

STYLE

What you and your family want from a garden will partly affect the style of garden you choose – from a relaxed, flowing style to formal symmetry, from open sweeps of green grass inviting family cricket games to an ever-surprising series of garden rooms.

Some popular styles include an informal garden with curves and natural lines and usually a large lawn; a formal garden with severely geometric lines, and often with walls, paths, steps and other structures; a cottage garden, free-flowing and generously planted; a Japanese garden with its typical oriental ornaments; and a Tuscan garden with earth-coloured walls and tall conifers. Choose a garden style that suits that of your house.

PLANNING

Buy a large, sturdy notebook, a few pages of graph paper, some tracing paper, pencil, eraser and coloured pencils and keep these in a box file with the exciting title of New Garden. As you plan, add useful pictures and cuttings from gardening maga-

ABOVE *A small wooden bench and two guinea fowl on a table set among leaves and flowers are an invitation to relax and admire the garden. The paving has been interplanted with feathery achillea.*

OPPOSITE PAGE *A touch of the orient is lent by the Japanese-style garden ornament and the elegantly clipped tree with its air of ancient serenity.*

zines or garden centre free-sheets to your file. If you live in a cluster-housing scheme or estate, consult your body corporate, to find out what you may or may not do.

There are probably limits to the range of walls or hedges permitted, as well as the choice of trees. Your levies may include some services such as the mowing of lawns, hedge-trimming and garden refuse removal. Your local municipality may also have restrictions affecting the planting of trees.

Check on your house plans to find out where and how deep the sewerage and water pipes are laid in the area that you are about to turn into a garden. It would be disastrous to dig down to make a hole for a tree or shrub, then suddenly hear a swish of water as you cut into a pipe.

Wherever you settle, get to know the neighbourhood. Take long walks around the area to look at other gardens and parks. Make notes of what you like and what thrives in your area.

If you are completely at sea as to how to deal with your new garden, it may pay you to bring in a landscaper, who can offer you several options of involvement. You may want an overall plan, a detailed plan, or you may think it worthwhile to ask the landscaper to take over the entire planning and planting. But before you do this, make absolutely sure of what you yourself want out of a garden. This may sound like an expensive operation, but it is a strange thing that homeowners will spend huge amounts of money on constructing a home, but not be willing to spend another two or three per cent on the garden.

BELOW *Here an unsympathetic, slab-like wall was softened by a custom-made metal arch structure and a strategically placed statue. The central arch is echoed by the perfectly circular lawn with its neat rim of lighter paving.*

ASPECT

Knowing the aspect of your garden, whether it faces north, south, east or west, will affect your planning.

Trace the path of the sun across your garden in winter and in summer. This is important, as the placing of a wall or building, or the planting of a tree could cut out the sun from your projected patio or pool. In the southern hemisphere, the sun 'goes north' in winter, then 'comes south' in summer. Thus, a wall running from east to west will receive sun on its northern side and shade on its southern side. In winter this will be more accentuated. Although the sun will come further south in summer, there will always be shade on the southern side of the wall. A wall running from north to south means that the plants on the eastern side will receive gentle morning sun, while those on the western side will be hot indeed in the afternoon sun.

When it comes to planting trees, in the colder garden it is usually wise to plant deciduous trees in the northern part of the garden, so there is shade in summer, but in winter, when the sun is in the north, the trees, bereft of leaves, will let the sun through to the ground below, allowing for planting of winter

and spring flowers. Most plants love the morning sun. But in frosty areas slightly tender plants which are affected by the frost will suffer in the early morning, whereas if they are away from the morning sun, they will be able to thaw out gradually.

Considerations of aspect are particularly important if you are planning to erect structures or plant large trees in your garden.

ABOVE A small garden has been given strongly structured paths made from sleepers and stepping stones interspersed with pebbles. The white of the pebbles is duplicated in the corner water feature.

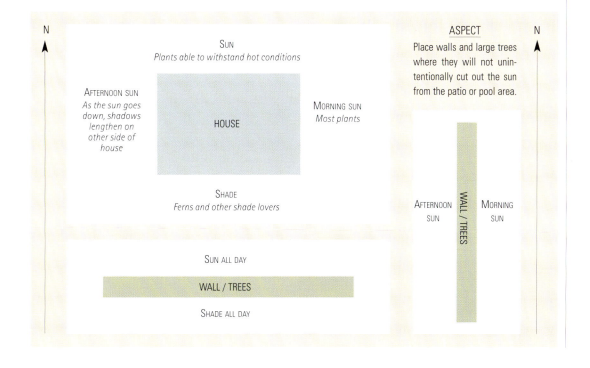

RIGHT *This attractive wall of four metres was actualy made from discarded car tyres which are freely available as they may not be thrown on the rubbish dump. Each tyre, laid brick-style, straddling the two below, is lined with plastic sheeting, filled with soil and planted.*

BELOW *One option for a slope is to make walled terraces, another is to make gently undulating slopes and plant them with grass and flowers. Wash-off of topsoil could be a danger, and precautions should be taken to avoid this.*

WIND DIRECTION

Wind can be highly destructive, so find out the direction of prevailing winds, then plant or build to keep them at bay. It might be well to bear in mind the fact that wind blowing over a wall will create small whirlpools of air, which is bad for the plants, whereas wind is dispersed more gently through several ranks of shrubs.

SLOPE

Which way does the land slope? Which way do you want it to slope? Towards or away from the sun, away from the wind? Getting the contours right will be the first chore, and this may involve earthmoving. Levelling an area by cutting and filling means taking soil from the upper part of the slope and using this to fill in the lower end. This may require building a retaining wall to keep up this lower end.

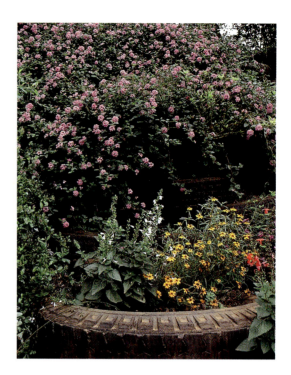

In making any alteration to levels, always put aside any topsoil for future use. You may need a contractor with an earthmoving machine to level areas, remove tree stumps or dense weed growth, but get him to bring the lightest model possible and avoid unnecessary compacting of the soil or burying of fertile topsoil.

You may prefer to retain the slope, in which case planting can go ahead without further ado. But do bear in mind that a grassed slope will be difficult to mow. In addition, if you create beds in this area you will have to build steps and paths for access and thirdly there is always the danger of losing precious topsoil through run-off of water. (*See* pages 136 – 137 for details of planting on slopes.)

STRUCTURES

Even the simplest garden plan will need some construction, whether it's just a boundary wall or a fence. However, you may want a swimming-pool with access paths or paving, a pergola, a patio or a wooden deck. You may even dream of a water feature. Turn to page 123 to consider some of the options. Then incorporate them in the garden plan you are ready to create.

YOUR 3-STAGE PLAN

Planning in three careful stages will help clarify your thinking about what you really want in that ideal garden, and where you want it.

Basic scale drawing

Measure your plot and the size and position of the house, driveway and other existing structures. Then draft a scale drawing of your property on graph paper. If you have access to your house building plans, just trace off the outline you need. Remember to add an arrow indicating 'north' so you can trace the sun's path. Also indicate prevailing winds, if these will be a factor. Sketch in any existing large trees, shrubs and boundary walls which will create shade, and mark damp or rocky areas.

Areas and structures

Now sketch, to scale, the functional areas and additional structures you intend to add (see page 21). Decide what you want to do in your garden, and where. Then items such as the entertainment area, a patio or patios, a swimming-pool, paths, children's play area, water feature, utility yard and garden shed can be sketched in. Your boundary is one of your first considerations, being perhaps a structure, perhaps part of the planting plan, perhaps a combination of both.

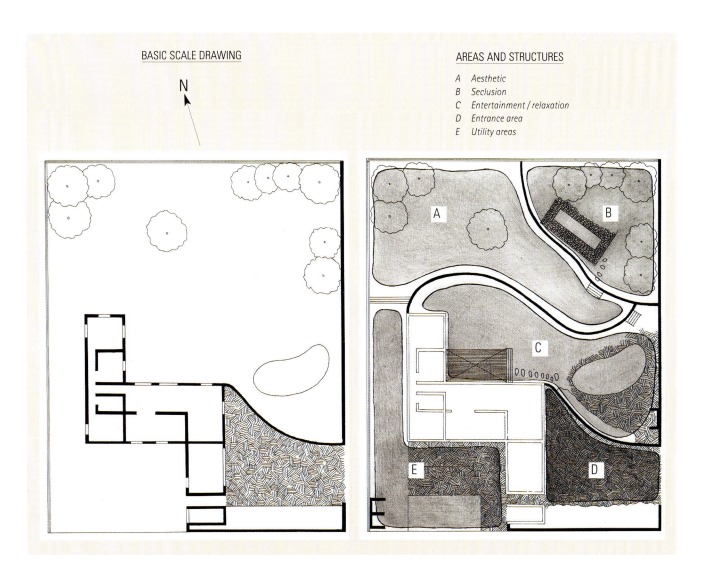

BASIC SCALE DRAWING

N

AREAS AND STRUCTURES

A   Aesthetic
B   Seclusion
C   Entertainment / relaxation
D   Entrance area
E   Utility areas

Planting plan

Here is where you play Mother Nature, sketching in, on an overlay of tracing paper, spreading trees, billowing shrubs and glorious flower beds. On the actual site, use the hose or a rope to outline proposed flower beds and place tall sticks and sun umbrellas to mark where trees are to be. You are probably going to make many plans before you are happy, so create several tracing paper overlays to try out various layouts and styles. The following sections will provide a wealth of suggestions about plants – and structures and features – which can be brought into both a new garden and an established one.

Renovating an established garden

If you bought your new home because of the beautiful garden, there is probably little to be done in the way of planning. However, if it was only the house you loved, then the garden may need a great deal of attention.

Above all, resist the urge to remove any plants which you think are unsightly or useless. New gardeners have been known to take out several shrubs which look like bunches of dead sticks, then come springtime, discover that the lovely flowering shrubs in full bloom at the local nursery are what they had rashly discarded! Find out all you can about your

PLANTING PLAN

A	Larger trees	H	Braai area
B	Water feature	I	Pot plants
C	Retaining wall	J	Flower bed
D	Steps	K	Herb garden
E	Deck / pergola	L	Compost
F	Swimming-pool	M	Rubbish
G	Seating	N	Fruit trees

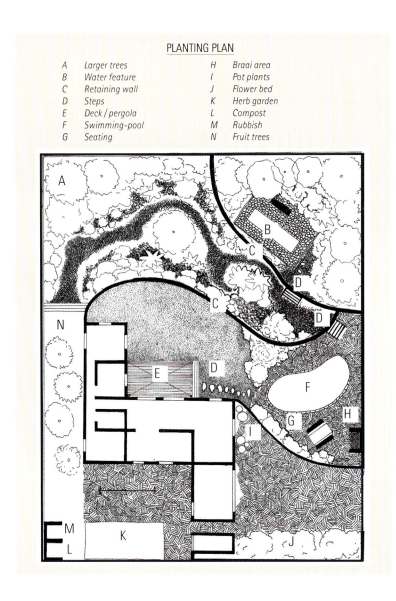

QUICK TIPS

- A view from window, patio or corner may be framed with foliage, or left open.
- If possible, have a view of the garden from every window of the house.
- You can borrow a view from adjacent open ground or gardens, cleverly disguising where your garden ends and the borrowed part begins. So think before you plant screening around every centimetre of your perimeter.
- Plant shrubs and climbers with lovely scents near outdoor seating areas.
- The area around the house should be level, and preferably paved, so it can be walked on after rain.
- Paths should be designed and placed with care. *See* page 22 for more detail.
- A path which narrows slightly as it recedes into the distance can give an illusion of length.
- A long narrow garden can be made to look shorter by placing a low wall or low hedge across the centre.
- The pool area should be free of water from neighbouring banks and walls. If it is lower than the general garden, make sure there are drains to take away excess water.
- A focal point can bring an entire picture together – for instance, a statue, a birdbath, a group of trees.
- In a formal garden, it is essential to keep the ground perfectly level, and beds geometrically laid out.
- Trees and shrubs planted along the border of a small garden will make it look larger.
- Until your garden is established, a few containers and hanging baskets planted with bright flowers placed close to the house will certainly create an impression of colour and fertility, a promise of the lovely garden in your future.

new garden from neighbours and the nearest garden centre. It may hold treasures which should be cherished.

Trees which spread themselves wide and low can have their lower branches cut away to allow light through. Untidy hedges can be clipped back. If the hedge has no growth at ground level, try bending side stems down low, making a few cuts on their underside and pinning the stems so that they touch the ground. This layering will produce new plants, thus filling out a sparse hedge.

Cut back unwanted branches from shrubs and trees. Clear paths and steps, making repairs if necessary. Take out every single weed, cut back spent perennials and mow the lawn. Now step back and look. That neglected garden may not be as bad as you originally thought. But a major overhaul may still be necessary. If so, take out those pencils and paper and start on your well-considered plan. Take your time, take frequent breaks, walk in the garden, get the feel of it, and give thanks for being where you are. Hurried decisions may result in long-term disappointments.

BELOW *Lavenders in the foreground give way to day lilies and pincushions, golden elder and a 'Swane's Gold' conifer. This bright and cheerful congregation of plants gathers together around a large terracotta jar which acts as a fine focal point.*

Boundaries & structures

The structures in your garden – around which the planting flows – must be chosen and positioned as an integral part of the plan you carefully draw up on your sketch pad. Whether they form boundaries, focal points, means of access or protection of some kind, you will want them to be both functional and beautiful. Structures may include trees and shrubs where they constitute the boundary definition.

Boundaries

As the frame which contains your garden (and often ensures your security) your boundaries – what you erect and what you plant there – will probably be the first thing to consider. Bear in mind that the path of the sun will affect your choice of planting (see page 13). Your boundaries will provide privacy, but will also cast shadow.

WALLS

If security is your most pressing need, then the answer is certainly a wall, which looks best blending with the house in materials and colour. While they provide privacy and security, walls are permanent and largely unchangeable, and can create spots of merciless heat detrimental to plants.

Walls create their own micro-climates in your garden. A solid wall, or one planted with a closely clinging creeper, will deflect any prevailing wind approaching from outside the garden, up and over the top of the wall. This causes turbulence on the garden side, possibly damaging nearby plants. Shrubs and trees planted close to the wall on the inner, garden side will disperse the wind to a great extent.

Temperatures are also affected. For instance, if a wall runs from north to south, the plants on the eastern side will receive the gentle morning sun whereas those on the western side will receive the hot afternoon sun. A wall running from east to west should have sun-loving plants on its northern side,

which is always in the sun, while shade-loving specimens will relish the permanent shade on the southern side. A climbing plant which is placed on the southern side of this wall will surely find its way up and over the wall, to bloom on the sunny northern side. A northfacing inside corner where two walls meet will be especially hot, as both walls reflect heat into the space.

A breeze-brick wall, one in which bricks are laid so there are regular open spaces, will let the air through into an otherwise hot garden area.

A rainshadow can also be created on the side of the wall facing away from the usual angle of the rain. (See pages 28 – 29 for more information on climate and micro-climates.)

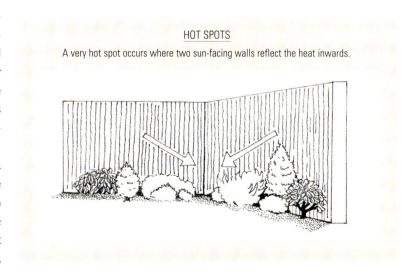

HOT SPOTS
A very hot spot occurs where two sun-facing walls reflect the heat inwards.

RIGHT *Trees arching
over a low hedge define
the garden boundary,
and make a perfect
frame for the view of
the main garden from
the driveway.*

To break up the monotony of a long wall, alcoves can be made to receive plants. Some sensitive tree-lovers even build a wall around the protruding branch or trunk of an established tree, with charming effect. Plant-boxes or ornaments can be suspended from a wall for a touch of colour. A moon gate set into a wall will not only give access to another section of the garden, but will also frame the view beyond. If you want to plant a clinging creeper to cover a wall, it is advisable to cover the relevant portion with wire mesh first, to avoid unsightly marks on the wall when one day you remove that creeper.

FENCES

Fences made from wooden slats or split poles look good, but are not very substantial or long-lasting. Wire-mesh fences appear uncompromisingly utilitarian, but can be effectively camouflaged with shrubs and creepers, resulting in a combination of security and a natural effect.

HEDGES

A well-maintained hedge is a good backdrop for any garden, and may be valued for its foliage alone or also for its flowers. A formal hedge will need constant attention to keep it looking good, but you could create an informal hedge from a carefully chosen mixture of shrubs, which would probably only need an annual pruning.

Here try to choose shrubs that grow at more or less the same rate, are all evergreen and do not have flowers of ill-matched colours. Hedges can be more effective windbreaks than walls, but their roots can invade adjacent flower beds.

To avoid wind deflecting upwards and creating turbulence on the other side, rather plant a hedge than build a wall, as even the densest hedge will allow some wind to filter through. Planting a few parallel rows varying in height is an excellent method of cutting down wind velocity. The extent to which wind is reduced depends on the height and breadth of the planting. The distance from the windbreak for which wind reduction persists, varies from five to ten times the height of the planting. (See pages 44 – 47 for details on planting, training and trimming hedges as well as suggestions for good hedge subjects.)

SHRUBS AND TREES

Planting a generous number of shrubs and trees on the border will be pleasing to the eye, will create a windbreak and will conceal the boundary, thus making the garden look bigger. Both on the boundary and within the garden, trees can be used to frame a view. Care should be taken to choose those which will not grow too tall, or which will not take up too much goodness from the neighbouring soil. As with any plants, when you buy a larger specimen, you are buying time. By choosing larger trees, shrubs and hedging plants, you are buying two, three or even more years' growth. Bear in mind that by planting groups of shrubs and trees, you will be creating a micro-climate in that part of the garden – such groups may create a protective windbreak, but other plants must be able to tolerate their shade.

Structures

These are the permanent features of the garden, and situation and materials should be carefully chosen. Ideally it is best to erect as many of the structures as soon as possible so that the rubble can be cleared away and the serious planting begin.

PERGOLAS AND ARCHES

The structure – both pillars and overhead support – must be strong and durable. Pillars of stone or brick are ideal, while overheads can be of wood or metal. Ensure that your structure is high enough to allow for thick foliage or flowers hanging down from overhead plants. Three metres is certainly not too high. An arch also makes a more impressive statement if it is wide enough for two people to pass under it side by side. It should be borne in mind that any climbing plant will go in search of the light, which means that those planted on the southern side will climb up and over to the northern side.

ABOVE The ouline of this classic urn, planted with a dark green ivy trained over wire, is echoed in a similar container further down the path.

LEFT 'Brilliant' bougainvillea has clothed its wall completely with vibrant colour – a beautiful boundary planting which is also a substantial deterrent to intruders.

If you do not have the time or the money to construct a pergola at once, it is wise to clear the space and then either pave it, remembering where the pillars are going to be, or enrich the soil and establish plants or ground covers.

NON-BOUNDARY WALLS

These may be used to enclose sections of the garden and are normally lower than the boundary walls. They are also often constructed to double up as narrow raised beds, with two walls built a short distance apart then filled with good soil and planted up. Walls are also constructed to retain the soil of terraces. Whatever the material used – bricks, stone or concrete – weepholes must be left at regular intervals to deal with excess water.

Under-foot structures

These must be both practical, attractive and suited to your style of garden.

PATHS

A path may be a no-nonsense straight line from A to B, or it can be an invitation to a journey, making the getting there an experience.

Paving stones come in a variety of shapes, sizes and colours, large enough to span the width of the path or small enough for intricate designs. Bricks, too, can be laid in all kinds of patterns. All of these need a base which has been compacted until solid and level. A layer of sand is then laid down, followed by the paving stones or bricks.

The gaps are filled with dry cement, brushed in and then sprinkled with water. If you want to plant in the spaces between pavers, enrich the soil with compost and fertilizer first.

Concrete paths are constructed by pouring wet concrete into wooden frames. Crazy paving, not seen much these days, needs careful laying because of the uneven thickness of the stones.

Flowing (non-fixed) materials include gravel and pine bark chips. These can be merely scattered over a level surface with an edging of bricks half-submerged lengthwise to stabilise the path. Gravel is however not a wise choice for the garden where small bare feet are likely to patter. An earth path can look charmingly natural, but can be slippery in wet weather. To deal with the mud, lay down pine

needles, pine bark or mulch. To stop the soil from nearby beds flowing on to the path, lay a row of low bricks or stones or a strip of concrete. Alternatively plant an edging of echeverias, violets, mondo grass or liriope.

Water run-off can be a problem on a sloping path, especially a plain concrete one. You could construct occasional humps to lead the water into channels at the side of the path, or leave a gap across the concrete at regular intervals, remove the soil to a good depth and fill the space with pebbles to take up the surplus water. Planting these spaces with low-growing plants would also help. A third and possibly best solution would be to include a few steps to interrupt the flow of water. A drain at the base of the steps can lead away excess water.

STEPS

Safety is of prime importance, for a wobbly tread can cause slips and spills. Steps may be laid in the traditional style, with the addition of a space at the back of each tread, filled with rich soil for planting and transformed into a pretty feature.

Wooden sleepers can be used to good effect, but they tend to retain dampness and become slippery in wet weather.

PAVING

In many gardens paving is being used to replace part of the lawn, or indeed the whole lawn. Thanks to the large variety of materials available, it is possible to turn paving into an attractive feature, with inter-plantings of low-growing plants, a judicious selection of containers, and perhaps a bench, a statue or even a small water feature.

A small level paved area in the shade of a tree is ideal for some comfortable seating.

There is a vast range of paving stones available, including special sets of cobble stones to create fan-shapes and interlocking paving stones ideal for areas of heavy traffic. Paving stones or slabs are laid out as for paths. Take great care to achieve a level surface, tapping each stone into place and checking it with a spirit level, to prevent tripping and accidents.

Leave a few spaces open for planting, as this will soften the effect.

WATER FEATURES

A pond of any size can make a wonderful focal point for your design. Ponds and water features are discussed on pages 122 – 129.

BELOW Log sections are joined together to form manageable squares, which are then laid down, saving the tedious task of laying down each and every one separately.

TIPS FOR PATHS
- Use logic when positioning a path. Work out where there is most traffic, and make sure paths lead to somewhere. They must be used and not avoided.
- Too many curves in a path will be a temptation to take short cuts.
- Make the path wide enough for two people to walk side by side, but this is not essential.
- If the path is the only access to the garden, then it should at least be wide enough to take a wheelbarrow.
- Paths in shady spots – or all paths in wet weather – can become slippery and dangerous. If algae and moss grow, wash the areas down with a copper sulphate solution, or scrub with soap and water.
- A sloping concrete path with a smooth surface could become dangerous in wet weather, so rather scarify the surface during construction to roughen it.
- A long straight path can be boring, so break its length by widening it enough to take a bird-bath, a fountain, a sun dial, a column or an urn.
- If a path is made across a stretch of lawn, make sure that the paving is just below the level of the lawn, so the mower can ride easily over it.

Environment

By now you will have drawn up an overall plan for your new garden and are probably eager to fill it with plants. But there are a few more vital factors which must be considered before you place a single plant in your garden. One of these is your environment, including your climate and your soil, that living, miraculous substance which will anchor the plants and give them sustenance.

Soil

With wise and loving attention, the soil will bring wonderful fertility to the garden. However, if neglected it will allow plants, which may have cost a great deal, to die. Take care of your soil and you will always have a garden of great beauty.

The fertile soil found in most gardens has taken many years to form and is a mixture of infinitesimal pieces of plant material, weathered rock and living organisms which occur near to the surface, together with air and water. In the field and forest, plants grow naturally year after year. Their dropped leaves form food for the mother plant and rain from the heavens above dissolves these, and other nutrients in the soil, into an absorbable form.

In our gardens, we plant annuals and perennials, which obligingly bloom. Then we take them out and replace them with others which we expect to grow in the now-impoverished soil. Replenishment of the soil before every planting is essential and should become routine. Before you plant anything in your garden, make sure the soil is as good as it can be.

WHAT KIND OF SOIL?

There are several aspects to soil. It may be acid or alkaline. This is described accurately as the pH of the soil, measured on a scale of one to 14. One to six is on the acid side, seven is neutral and numbers above that indicate rising alkalinity. Acid soil occurs where rainfall is high, the rain having leached out some of the chemicals. This occurs in cooler parts and supports such plants as azaleas, rhododendrons, ericas and others. In fact they will not tolerate lime in the soil. Alkaline soil occurs in the drier parts and supports a vast array of plants.

The texture of soil is also vital. It may be heavy clay, which is often extremely fertile but has very small particles which stick together, excluding air and easily becoming water-logged. It may be light, sandy soil, easy to work but lacking nutrients or the ability to retain water. It may be a good loam, rich in humus. Find out what kind of soil you have by consulting your garden centre or agricultural centre and act accordingly.

ABOVE *Sub-tropical gardeners grow an enormous range of foliage plants in their warm and humid gardens. Relishing the shade in a Durban garden are richly coloured caladiums and crotons with green syngoniums and palm leaves, and an edging of* Pilea microphylla.

OPPOSITE PAGE *In high rainfall areas the soil is acid an nourishes such plants as azaleas and camellias. Here a tall* Pieris forrestii *still has some of its new pink leaves and its flowers which resemble lily of the valley. The pink azalea, purple* Iris sibirica *and pieris all demand acid soil. Even the oxalis at the edge will keel over if lime is sprinkled into its centre.*

LEFT *Crotons, acalyphas ferns, dracaenas and palm trees are completely at home where the air is humid and warm, and frost is unknown.*

There are also three levels of soil: topsoil, usually darker brown, richer in organic matter and the best growing medium; sub-soil, lighter in colour with fewer nutrients and organic matter; and the bedrock beneath. Ensure that careless digging does not bury your precious topsoil underneath the sub-soil.

Gardeners are forever wanting to grow plants which are not really suitable to the soil in their gardens. For example they plant azaleas in an alkaline soil, adding acid compost and sprinkling aluminium sulphate around them. This works for a certain time, but will remain a constant battle.

Surely it is better to plant something more suitable which will flourish with ease.

HOW TO IMPROVE YOUR SOIL

You can change the quality and texture of your soil by adding organic material and chemical fertilizers and by mixing different kinds of soil together. Both clay and sand can be improved by the addition of copious amounts of compost. The texture of clay will benefit from being mixed with sand to help break it down.

Organic material

Compost and other organic material, including kraal manure, chicken manure, stable litter and leafmould will not only give the soil a much more efficient texture, but will also provide nutrients for the plants.

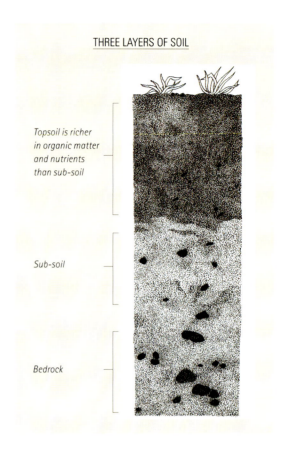

THREE LAYERS OF SOIL

Topsoil is richer in organic matter and nutrients than sub-soil

Sub-soil

Bedrock

Compost-making is simple and very effective. It merely consists of alternating layers of coarse, twiggy material with layers of finer clippings and cuttings and kitchen waste such as vegetable and fruit peel, eggshells and used tea-leaves. If clippings are too coarse, lay them on the ground and cut them up with a cane knife or machete. However if you often have plenty of pruned branches, a power mulcher-machine is a wonderful investment as it reduces the trimmings to small, decomposable pieces effortlessly. Include a layer of activator powder or manure and top it with a layer of soil. Water the compost heap in dry weather. Keeping a compost heap going is eco-friendly and provides a constant supply of wonderful nutrition.

Never burn fallen leaves. Place them in black plastic bags with a little water and a few air holes and make your own leafmould which is excellent for enriching the soil. Leaves take longer than garden clippings to decompose and are best left on their own to break down.

MAKING YOUR OWN COMPOST HEAP

Soil
Manure

Kitchen waste

Finer clippings

Coarse twigs and straw

CHEMICAL FERTILIZERS

Apart from organic material, there are chemicals which are taken up readily by plants. NPK are the symbols for the chemicals you will find on certain bags of chemical fertilizer. They stand for Nitrogen, Phosphorus and Potassium.

These chemicals are mixed in different ratios according to the needs of various plants. They are always identified in this order and are numbered according to their proportions, such as 2:3:2 or 8:1:5. Added to this is another number in brackets, which stands for the percentage of those chemicals in the overall mix.

- Nitrogen is essential to all plants and especially for the development of leaves. It is used extensively for green vegetables, but recently a fertiliser with plenty of nitrogen has come to be appreciated by rose growers and others who know the value of healthy foliage.
- Phosphorus promotes healthy growth of flowers, fruit and roots. Superphosphate is a chemical form of phosphorus, while bonemeal is a natural source. Superphosphate is useful for acid soils which often lack phosphates.

- Potassium helps plants combat disease. Potatoes and root crops absorb large quantities of potassium.
- A good general fertilizer is 2:3:2 or 2:3:4, while for roses 3:1:5, 5:1:5 and even 8:1:5 are used to produce a healthy crop of leaves. Use 4:1:1 for greening an already well-established lawn well into the growing season.
- LAN (limestone ammonium nitrate) yields mostly nitrogen, but has other beneficial effects, for example it can make clay less sticky and more porous.

There are also supplements available to add manganese, molybdenum and other trace elements. If you suspect a plant is lacking one of these, take a leaf into your garden centre and ask for advice.

TIPS FOR SOIL IMPROVEMENT

- Improvement agents such as gypsum or lime can be used to break open compacted soil to allow water to penetrate.
- At all times there should be a mulch on the soil surface — that is, a layer of organic material, which will keep the soil moist. This can be compost, peanut shells, other nut shells, pine needles or other leaves.
- Slow-release fertiliser is what it says — it releases the nutrients slowly and steadily, and will not burn plants. A slow-release fertiliser may be laid down on the lawn when it is dry, and be activated only when it rains.
- Liquid manure can be made by hanging sacks of chicken or kraal manure in a barrel of water, then using the liquid when it has reached the colour of weak tea.
- Seaweed manure (Seagro or Kelpak) is used in liquid form and can be applied to the soil or used as a foliar feed sprayed directly on to the leaves.
- Don't apply lime at the same time as manure, but definitely wait a few weeks.

BELOW *Hydrangeas, a lovely part of the summer scene in the garden, are cherished in most parts of the country. Their colouration depends greatly on the soil type. Generally acid soil produces blue flowers and alkaline soil produces pink flowers. Hydrangea macrophylla are divided into the 'Lacecaps' which have a mass of fertile flowers in the centre; and the 'Hortensias', with their great rounded heads of sterile flowers.*

Climate

Depending on its climate and other factors, your area will fall into one of eight natural communities of flora and fauna. You could be gardening in one of the winter rainfall areas: Fynbos, the Strandveld, or the Succulent Karoo; or in one of the summer rainfall areas: the Forest (the Sub-tropical Forest or the Afro-temperate Forest of the Garden Route and other scattered pockets), the Bushveld, the Thicket, the Karoo or the Grasslands region.

OUR NATURAL REGIONS

In these various regions different plants flourish. Take your cue from the successful indigenous plants in your area. (*See* pages 76 – 83 for details on gardening with indigenous plants.)

In areas with cold, frosty winters herbaceous plants are able to die down and rest when the cold weather comes, then come into new life with the warming of spring.

Wet winters, such as those experienced in the Western Cape with its Mediterranean climate, bring bulbs and indigenous annuals into full bloom in spring, whereafter they die down during the dry summer. This is why when you plant Cape bulbs in summer rainfall regions it is best to lift them after blooming to allow them to escape the heavy rains that follow.

In sub-tropical regions there is year-round warmth and humidity, with a slight cooling in winter. This is where colourful foliage plants and highly coloured flowers thrive.

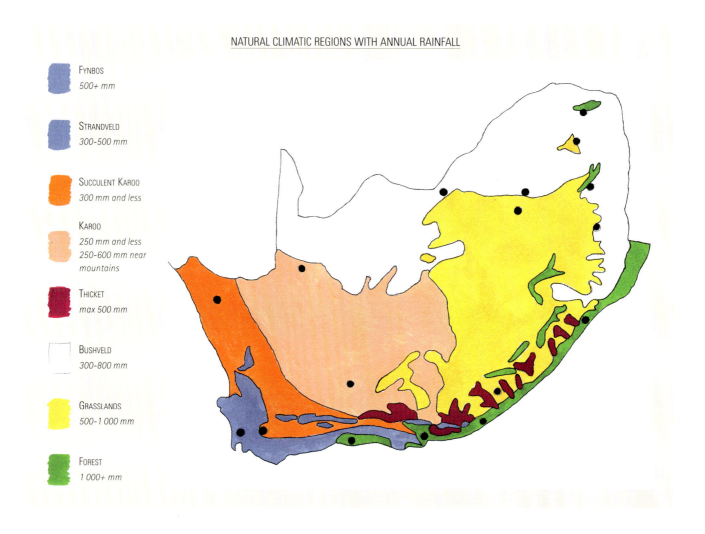

NATURAL CLIMATIC REGIONS WITH ANNUAL RAINFALL

FYNBOS
500+ mm

STRANDVELD
300-500 mm

SUCCULENT KAROO
300 mm and less

KAROO
250 mm and less
250-600 mm near mountains

THICKET
max 500 mm

BUSHVELD
300-800 mm

GRASSLANDS
500-1 000 mm

FOREST
1 000+ mm

Examples of these are the crotons *(Codiaeum spp.),* acalyphas, dieffenbachias and marantas.

In parts with severely dry, cold winters the well-adapted indigenous plants come into their own, in the veld and in the gardens. If you garden in a hot, dry area, read the advice on page 134. Mulching, watering, shading and protecting can certainly help in the more challenging climatic regions.

Frost-prone areas require special gardening know-how. Only hardy plants should be chosen for winter. Plant only the toughest specimens in those spots in your garden which are particularly vulnerable to frost. When pruning, don't cut back plants that are frost-bitten, as this could encourage tender new growth which would be destroyed by the next frost. Rather wait until all frost is over. Also take special precautions with regard to protection and watering (see page 152).

Often gardeners in the colder inland regions hanker after the colourful foliage of acalyphas and crotons, whereas the warm climate gardeners would love to grow the primulas and daffodils that thrive in the temperate regions. But wherever you live in South Africa, there is a wealth of plants which will grow under your particular conditions and, in fact, do well with a little added attention to soil and water supply. You can also expand your range of plants by using containers, as they can be moved about when the weather changes.

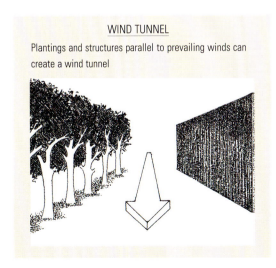

WIND TUNNEL

Plantings and structures parallel to prevailing winds can create a wind tunnel

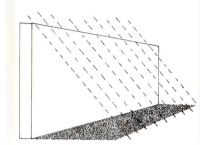

RAIN SHADOWS

Walls and trees can create a rainshadow. Allow for this when taking care of your plants' watering needs.

GARDEN MICRO-CLIMATES

Various structures, trees and large shrubs, combined with aspect and prevailing winds, can create quite distinct micro-climates in different parts of your garden. Beware of creating wind tunnels when you position new structures or plant new trees or hedges, as these force wind through at speed, damaging plants in its path.

As cold air is heavier than warm, frost will settle in low dips in the garden and sometimes behind blockages like walls or hedges, so plant only hardy specimens here. Frost damage is lower in gardens where the air can circulate freely and where the soil drains well. Frost cover is available in the form of an extremely light fabric which virtually floats above plants, keeping frost at bay.

Dazzling white walls will reflect light on to plants, which can be useful in a slightly shady position, but damaging in the full glare of the summer afternoon sun. A brick wall which absorbs heat during the day will release it overnight, keeping a nearby plant warmer than those further away.

Ground-level surfaces also create micro-climates. A tarred driveway absorbs heat, but a path paved with light stones will reflect heat. Lawns too, absorb heat. Water has its own particular effect. A swimming-pool evens out the extremes of temperature in the air around it and all water reflects light, to the benefit of sun-loving plants.

Plants for your garden

At last it's time for planting! And what an array of plants there is to choose from. Every year plant breeders bring exciting new varieties on to the market – new colours, variegations and sizes of shrubs; new and exciting varieties of perennials and annuals. Just think of pansies alone. What a huge diversity there is of this lovely winter and spring bloomer, with new colours coming along each season. Explore what is available, look at other people's gardens and visit commercial plant nurseries.

The beautiful profusion of spring is evident from a glorious gathering of flowering trees, shrubs, perennials and annuals. A flowering cherry (Prunus serrulata) *in full spring array has a living carpet of pink* Bellis perennis *and blue* Phlox divaricata *beneath it, while beyond, in rather startling contrast, a deciduous azalea is covered in flowers of burnt orange.*

Trees

Of all garden plants, trees take the longest to grow and develop, so it is best to plant them as soon as possible. But don't rush your choice, as they will be there for a long time, and, when they reach maturity, they will not be easy to remove. Also consider their eventual size and avoid overcrowding which may spoil or conceal natural shapes and lead to stunted growth.

Trees enhance your garden

Trees may be giants, hundreds of feet high and wide-spreading, or they may be low and slender. Trees can bring colour and structure, they can make a statement. They bring welcome shade in the summer, they bring seclusion and provide a soft, natural way to hide an unsightly view. A tree will filter dust blowing across from a dirt-road and can also muffle noise. A tree in your garden will be there for most of your life, and you will come to regard it as a personal friend. Choose wisely and give it a good start, so that you can awake every morning, look out on your special tree or trees, and greet the community of wild life which has taken up residence there.

Size

Suit the eventual size of your tree to the scale of your garden. A thoughtful gardener plans for posterity and will avoid planting an overlarge tree which may some day be someone else's problem, to be cut down and leave the garden bare and bereft. Also ask how fast it will grow, especially if you need privacy or shade fairly quickly.

Bear in mind that some fast-growing trees can deplete the soil all round them, are more vulnerable to being knocked over by strong winds and do not live as long as slow-growers.

Trees also extend design possibilities in small and paved gardens by adding height and structure.

ABOVE *Senna fistula (syn. Cassia fistula) has often been compared to the laburnum tree, with its long trusses of golden flowers. This is essentially a tree for the warm garden, bringing its oppulent clear gold to the summer scene.*

OPPOSITE PAGE *The leaves of Acer negundo variegatum are in light-hearted contrast to the dark thatched roof. It has an array of roses, pentas and Inca lilies at its feet and will later lose its leaves, to allow the sun into the winter and early spring garden.*

LEFT *Albizia adianthifolia, the well-known, well-loved flatcrown tree, is well named for its habit of spreading wide its branches and stems with finely divided leaves. It can grow up to nearly 20 m tall with an almost equal spread, and makes a superb specimen tree in the larger garden.*

What kind of tree?

A tree may offer lovely foliage or attractive flowers, or even both. Cherries *(Prunus serrulata)* produce a froth of blossom in spring in colder areas, and in the warm sub-tropical gardens of KwaZulu-Natal and Mpumalanga there are yellow and pink cassias and tibouchinas, which bring splendid colour from late spring through to autumn. Among the indigenous beauties are September bells *(Rothmannia globosa)*, the Cape chestnut *(Calodendrum capense)* and the pompon tree *(Dais cotinifolia)*.

What about the shape of your tree. Do you want a spreading tree for shade or for blotting out an unsightly view? Or perhaps a tall slender conifer as a focal point? Imagine the lovely sculptural effects you could achieve by combining a few of these tree shapes: umbrella, conical, columnar, rounded, weeping and spreading.

You may want a deciduous tree, which will have an abundance of leaves in summer, change to vibrant colours in autumn, then lose all its leaves to let the sun through in winter, showing its majestic form, its tracery of branches and stems, during the cold months. Deciduous trees relish the colder areas, where winter cold will give them a seasonal rest. Among the larger trees with lovely autumn colours are maples *(Acer spp.)*, oaks *(Quercus spp.)*, planes *(Platanus x acerifolia)*, the tulip tree *(Liriodendron tulipifera)*, the swamp cypress *(Taxodium distichum)* and the liquidamber.

Smaller autumn beauties include the pride of India *(Lagerstroemia indica)*; the crab-apple *(Malus spp.)*,

BELOW *Acer palmatum atropurpurea, with its richly coloured indented leaves, contrasts strikingly with the pale pink blossoms of the flowering cherry* (Prunus serrulata) *beyond, to create a spring tapestry.*

grown for its spring flowers as well as autumn berries; the ancient *Ginkgo biloba*; flowering dogwood (*Cornus florida*); silver birches (*Betula pendula*); and the golden rain tree (*Koelreuteria paniculata*).

Evergreen trees may provide welcome foliage year-round, but this does not mean they never lose their leaves. It is an ongoing process throughout the year. Good choices are the false olive (*Buddleja saligna*), the golden cypress (*Chamaecyparis obtusa* 'Crippsii'), the wild plum (*Harpephyllum caffrum*), also good for coastal planting for its tolerance of salt air and wind, Cape holly (*Ilex mitis*), wild gardenias (*Rothmannia capensis*), and the umbrella tree (*Schefflera actinophylla*). The glossy leaves of the fiddlewood (*Citharexylum quadrangulare*) are green only in winter, but yellow, orange and gold from spring to autumn.

Don't forget the virtues of a fruit tree. Consider planting an orange or lemon tree next to your patio. It adds the glowing colour of its fruit to the winter scene for many months, after bearing blossoms with that typically heady fragrance.

One apple tree will produce enough fruit to be eaten fresh, stewed and bottled. A plum, peach or apricot tree will do the same. These are all deciduous and need a cold winter.

There are also many palm trees for the garden, too numerous to list here, and it is wise to obtain advice from your garden centre.

TIPS ON BUYING A TREE
- Make sure that it has a healthy crop of leaves with no dead side stems, and that roots have not grown through the bottom of the container.
- Check that it is well-established in its container and not recently planted, by giving it a gentle tug.
- Find a specimen that is well-branched and has plenty of new buds and shoots.
- Check the underside of the leaves to make sure that there is no sign of pests or diseases.
- Ensure that it is not on the list of invasive or otherwise undesirable aliens. The jacaranda for example, lovely as it is, may no longer be grown in our gardens.

The right position

To make sure that a tree will not shade all your flower beds, use a sun umbrella or long stick to estimate the eventual reach of its shadow, when mature, before you plant it.

An evergreen tree close to the house will make the rooms on that side dark, while too dense foliage near the swimming-pool will keep the water uncomfortably chilly. Bear in mind that trees with invasive roots could damage foundations, water or sewage pipes. Trees which can create root problems include the rubber tree (*Ficus elastica*), *Ficus nitida* and willows. Some – like the Lombardy poplar (*Populus nigra* 'Italica') and the false acacia (*Robinia pseudoacacia*) – send out invasive suckers.

A tree's surface roots could also make underplanting rather difficult.

Deciduous trees are not suitable when essential screening is needed for privacy, as they will leave you exposed in winter. But they can be useful planted north of the patio for summer shade over a much-used outdoor entertainment area.

BELOW *Stark and majestic against the African sky,* Kigelia africana, *the well-known sausage tree, is unique in its strange long, sausage-like fruits which arise from the deep crimson flowers. It needs plenty of space, and being a resident of the bushveld, will not live where frost is heavy.*

How to plant a tree

OPPOSITE PAGE LEFT
The tall and slender
Tabebuia chrysotricha,
with crimson Kalanchoe
blossfeldiana *at its feet,
provide a blaze of
colour. Each also asserts
its shape and texture
within the overall pic-
ture. The tabebuia loses
its leaves in winter, and
will not take heavy frost.*

OPPOSITE PAGE RIGHT
*Tibouchinas were
brought to the Natal
coast during the last
century, where they
found the soil and cli-
mate much to their lik-
ing. Now, they bloom in
unbelievable brilliance
where there is no dan-
ger of frost, covering
themselves with sump-
tuous purple, and vari-
ous shades of pink and
mauve. The can take on
a fairly untidy look, and
most gardeners like to
cut back one side at a
time, to make for denser
growth.*

OPPOSITE PAGE BOX
Bauhinia blakeana *is
surely the most out-
standing of this family
of trees. They have a
very long flowering
period, and gardeners
are coming to appreci-
ate its habit of still carrying flowers long after
the blossom trees have
finished. Its flowers
have an exotic look,
giving it its common
name of Hong Kong
orchid tree.*

Give your tree a good start by digging a hole about twice the size of the root ball, certainly no smaller than 60 cm square by 60 cm deep. Make the hole square, not round, so that the roots will search out the corners and penetrate into the surrounding soil, not just go around and around the hole. If the soil is dry, fill the hole with water and let it drain away before planting. Keep back the precious top soil and mix this with about a third in volume of compost or well-rotted kraal manure and one or more good handfuls of bonemeal. In heavy soils, loosen the bot-tom of the hole, then cover this with leafmould, straw, cinders or gravel, to ensure good drainage. In sandy soil, place leafmould, or even torn-up news-paper in the bottom, to make sure the water does not drain away too fast.

If the tree is in a bag of loose soil which may well fall away when the bag is removed, rather place the entire bag in the hole, then gently slit its sides. If the soil is very loose, slit the bottom too, do not remove the bag, but allow the roots to find their way through the slits.

Place the tree so that when planted its soil level will be exactly the same as it was in the container. A stick placed across the hole, to which the new tree is lightly tied, is useful in keeping it steady while fill-ing the hole. Fill the hole with the prepared soil, then gently firm it, so there is little subsidence. A stake may be necessary to keep the new tree upright and should be inserted in the hole at planting time. Don't tie the tree directly to the stake, but make a

figure of eight, looping the twine through a piece of tyre rubber or leather and ensuring that only this gentler material touches the tree trunk.

Water your newly planted tree well and give it a mulch of organic material, not touching the trunk. Continue to water well (about 50 litres) twice a week during the growing season especially in hot weather, once a week otherwise, until the tree is well-established. When it has reached this stage and is flourishing, give monthly applications of 2:3:2, not near the trunk, followed by a good drenching. Do not feed deciduous trees in winter.

If there are side stems close to the ground, remove these with a clean cut – they will be over-shadowed by the higher branches and will in any case probably be removed later on.

Some trees look lovely when they are allowed to drop their skirts to the lawn – the pin oak is just one of these, but this limits the area available in the gar-den, and it is often better to remove the lower branches, so there is high shade with good light but not direct sunlight. This should be done gradually, so there are no mistakes which cannot be rectified.

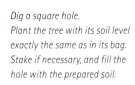

*Dig a square hole.
Plant the tree with its soil level
exactly the same as in its bag.
Stake if necessary, and fill the
hole with the prepared soil.*

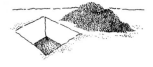

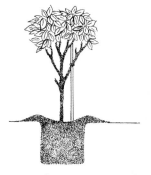

Pruning

On the whole, trees do not need pruning, except to tidy up their appearance. Flowering trees should be pruned immediately after flowering, if necessary, and some are also best trimmed when young to produce sturdy, compact heads. (*See pages 159 – 162 for more details.*)

INDIGENOUS TREES	OTHER POPULAR GARDEN TREES
Acacia karroo (sweet thorn)	*Arbutus unedo* (strawberry tree)
Alberta magna (Natal flame bush)	*Colvillea racemosa* (colville's glory)
Bolusanthus speciosus (tree wisteria)	*Magnolia grandiflora* (tree magnolia)
Celtis africana (white stinkwood)	*Pittosporum eugenioides* (lemonwood)
Combretum erythrophyllum (river bushwillow)	*Pittosporum tenuifolium*
Cussonia paniculata (mountain cabbage tree)	*Tibouchina spp.*
C. spicata (common cabbage tree)	
Ekebergia capensis (Cape ash)	
Erythrina lysistemon (coral tree)	
Ficus sur (broomcluster fig)	
Kigelia africana (sausage tree)	
Nuxia floribunda (forest elder)	
Olea europaea x africana (wild olive)	
Pittosporum viridiflorum (cheesewood)	
Rhus lancea (karee)	
Schotia brachypetala (tree fuchsia)	
Tarchonanthus camphoratus (wild camphor)	

Shrubs & climbers

Shrubs come in a huge diversity of shapes, colours and sizes. There are those which serve useful purposes in boundaries or windbreaks; those with lovely, sculptural shapes; those with unusual foliage or welcome flowers. They can bring seclusion and a certain amount of shade, whether planted as specimens, used in formal or informal hedges or even in border planting.

Size and shape

Shrubs range from low-growing to two or three metres high. Many, because of their dwarf growth, are highly suited to cultivation in the mixed border. There are evergreen shrubs which keep their green or variegated colours throughout the year, and deciduous shrubs which often have vivid colours in autumn.

As with trees, they are to be long-time residents in your garden, which means firstly that they should be carefully chosen, and secondly that they be given a good start in life. Because of their large range of colour, shape and foliage texture, shrubs can be grouped together in attractive compositions. So take your time and choose with care.

Foliage

Interesting foliage is gaining in importance as the demand for low-maintenance gardens grows, and hybridists have been paying special attention to shrubs with attractive leaves, whether they be green, coloured or variegated, with spots, blotches, stripes or margins of contrasting colours.

So striking are these colourful shrubs that it is possible to create groups whose colours blend or contrast to beautiful effect.

FOLIAGE

VARIEGATED FOLIAGE

Abutilon pictum 'Thompsonii' (variegated Chinese lantern)
Acalypha spp.
Aucuba japonica 'Crotonifolia' (Japanese laurel)
Berberis thunbergii 'Rose Glow'
Coprosma repens (mirror bush)
Codiaeum variegatum (croton)
Dracaena spp. (dragon tree)
Elaeagnus spp.
Furcraea selloa 'Marginata' (variegated false agave)
Hibiscus rosa-sinensis 'Cooperi' (variegated hibiscus)
Hypericum x moserianum 'Tricolor'
Ilex spp. (holly)
Phormium spp.

PURPLE OR MAROON FOLIAGE

Berberis thunbergii 'Atropurpurea'
Dodonaea angustifolia 'Purpurea' (purple hop bush)
Strobilanthes anisophyllus

GOLD FOLIAGE

Abelia x grandiflora 'Francis Mason'
Berberis thunbergii 'Aurea'
Coleonema album (confetti bush)
Codiaeum variegatum (croton)
Duranta erecta 'Sheena's Gold'
Euonymus japonicus 'Aureus'
Melaleuca bracteata 'Johannesburg Gold'

SILVER/GREY FOLIAGE

Leucadendron spp. (cone flower)
Santolina chamaecyparissus (lavender cotton)

GREEN FOLIAGE

Agave attenuata (dragon tree)
Camellia spp.
Colocasia spp. (elephant's ear)
Schefflera arboricola (Hawaiian elf)

You could even bring the different varieties within one family of plants together to make combinations of great interest. Think of the coprosmas, with their shining leaves, some of plain green, some with silver or gold margins, some even coffee-coloured. Then there are the crotons and acalyphas for the warm gardens, with their highly coloured foliage. And what of the conifers, with their vast range of colours and striking shapes. The advantage of grouping different members of shrub families together is that they all like the same growing conditions.

Apart from variegated leaves, there are those of one specific colour, such as the burgundy leaves of *Berberis thunbergii* 'Rose Glow' or the clear gold foliage of *Duranta erecta* 'Sheena's Gold'.

Green graces the garden with so many shades – from soft grey-green through yellow-green to the dark brooding green of camellias – that it is possible to create a subtle composition solely with green-foliaged shrubs.

Frost-resistant shrubs

Frost-resistant shrubs valued for their foliage are *Euonymus japonicus* 'Microphyllus Gold Dust' (clear yellow, low-growing), *E. fortunei* 'Emerald Gaiety' (bright green), *Calluna vulgaris* 'Gold Haze' (common heather with finely divided foliage in an unusual shade of gold), *Leptospermum scoparium* 'Cherry Brandy' (tea bush – a rounded bush with deep bronze foliage and red flowers in spring), *Nandina domestica* 'Pygmaea' (dwarf sacred bamboo, which keeps its scarlet leaves into early winter), several *Phormium spp.* (flax, with strap-like leaves of varying colours and variegated colour combinations) and *Elaeagnus pungens* 'Maculata' (with a splash of gold on its green leaves).

Berry-bearing shrubs

In autumn and winter, berries bring a bright glow to the garden and a rich source of food to appreciative birds. Cotoneasters carry their berries on long, arch-ing, thornless stems and have the extra advantage of leaves with warm autumn tints.

Pyracanthas or firethorns bear masses of vivid yel-low-orange or red berries. Because they have many thorns, they make good, secure hedges. (Note that *Pyracantha angustifolia*, of Chinese origin, has been declared an invader and may no longer be planted.)

Try *Crataegus x grignionensis* and *C. pubescens*. *Crataegus x lavallei* 'Carrierei' is a hardy shrub whose masses of white spring flowers are followed by bright red berries in autumn and winter. Prune berry-bearing shrubs immediately after the berries come to an end. (See pages 159 – 162 for more details on pruning.)

Flowering shrubs

It is a never-failing seasonal joy to see the buds on flowering shrubs unfolding into blooms of great beauty. There are so many of these shrubs to choose from. Climate will naturally affect your choice, as will the soil – its depth and texture, its acidity or alkalinity. Azaleas, for instance, simply must have acid soil, and will keel over in the presence of lime. The colour of showy hydrangeas depends on whether they are grown in acid or alkaline soil.

Many of the shrubs in local gardens are officially exotics, that is, they originally came from across distant seas, brought by amateur botanists, devoted gardeners and entrepreneurs over the years. There are so many truly glamorous beauties available today – from the hibiscus to the poinsettia, from the fuchsia to the double oleander – that it is possible to have shrubs flowering all through the year. Do ensure that your climate approximates that of their original home for them to perform at their best.

BELOW *Azaleas (Rhododendron indicum) announce the spring with their multitude of luminous flowers. They must have an acid soil and a good mulch to protect the feeding roots which are close to the surface of the soil.*

RIGHT *After losing its leaves,* Euphorbia pul-cherrima *(poinsettia) brings its brilliant scarlet (or pink, cream or yellow) colour to gardens where winters are mild. It likes full sun and just enough water to keep it going. Highly coloured leaf-like bracts surround the insignificant flowers.*

FAR RIGHT *Hydrangeas or Christmas flowers flourish in shade and semi-shade during the hot months, and need plenty of mulch and water.* Hydrangea macrophylla *'Lacecap' has fertile flowers surrounded by infertile florets.*

BELOW RIGHT *Camellia sasanqua are the first of this glamorous family of shrubs to bloom, from as early as March and April. Their foliage is smaller than that of the japonicas and reticulatas, and they make good hedging plants.*

A large proportion of shrubs, especially those indigenous to cold climates, are deciduous and bear their flowers on bare branches before the leaves appear, sometimes in spectacular displays. Viburnums, almonds and magnolias are among these, and play a wonderful part in late winter and early spring. In warmer regions evergreens are the order of the day, with leaves borne year-round and flowers in season. Knowing what colour the blooms are going to be, will help you make pleasing combinations. Think of a pure white camellia with pink primulas at its feet, or a scarlet *Clerodendrum splendens* encircled by white daisies.

If flowering shrubs need to be pruned, this should be done immediately after flowering. If you want to use blossoms for the vase, pick them when they are in full bud and place them in tepid water where they will open beautifully.

FLOWERING SHRUBS

Abelia spp.	*Gardenia augusta*
Abutilon x hybrids (Chinese lantern)	*Grevillea x hybrids*
Allamanda cathartica (shrubby alamanda)	*Heliotropium arborescens* (cherry pie)
Buddleja spp.	*Hibiscus rosa-sinensis*
Callistemon citrinus (bottlebrush)	*Ixora coccinea* (flame of the woods)
Cassia artemisioides syn. *Senna artemisioides* (silver cassia)	*Hydrangea spp.*
	Magnolia spp.
Cassia corymbosa syn. *Senna corymbosa*	*Murraya exotica* (orange jasmine)
Camellia spp.	*Pimelea rosea*
Cuphea spp.	*Rhododendron spp.* (azaleas)
Deutzia scabra (bridal wreath)	*Spiraea spp.*
Euphorbia pulcherrima (poinsettia)	*Streptosolen jamesonii* (marmalade bush)
Forsythia spp.	*Tibouchina spp.*
Fuchsias	*Viburnum spp.*

Conifers

There is such a vast range of conifers available that it is almost impossible to mention them all by name. With colours ranging from various shades of green through clear gold to grey-green with a purple tinge, they can blend or contrast with other plants, or make a colourful group on their own. Many conifers change colour in winter, making them extremely valuable in the cold months. The low-growing *Juniperus horizontalis* 'Plumosa' changes to purple in winter and is often chosen for its lovely colour.

The interesting, sculptural shapes of conifers are among their other great features. You can create a focal point with a single columnar cypress – or make a lovely composition with a group of slender, conical, rounded and spreading conifers. Add to this the fact that nearly all conifers are frost-hardy, and it will be obvious why they are among the most valued garden and container plants. Ask your garden centre which do best in your area, and buy according to your needs – be it for container plants, specimens, windbreaks, hedges or attractive groups.

Conifers need to be watered regularly and their roots kept cool with a layer of mulch, especially during hot weather. They like well-drained soil but must have moisture at all times.

ABOVE *Conifers are invaluable in the frosty garden, where they keep their colour and even strengthen it during winter. In summer, as is shown in this picture, the gold of the conifers is highlighted by the Lysimachia nummularia (creeping Jenny) ground cover, while the Dasylirion glaucophyllum asserts itself with its long spiky leaves.*

CONIFER SHAPES & COLOURS

TALL, SLENDER

Cupressus sempervirens 'Swane's Gold' (golden-yellow)

Juniperus scopulorum 'Skyrocket' (blue-grey)

PYRAMIDAL

Thuja occidentalis 'Smaragd' (rich green, good container subject)

COMPACT, DWARF

Cryptomeria japonica 'Vilmoriniana' (vivid green turning purple in winter)

Platycladus orientalis 'Aurea Nana Compacta' (golden-green turning gold in winter)

GLOBOSE

Thuja occidentalis 'Sunkist Gold' (gold)

ROUNDED

Chamaecyparis lawsoniana 'Tamariscifolia' (greyish-green, fern-like)

Thuja occidentalis 'Rheingold' (green turning to gold and bronze in autumn)

CONICAL

Chamaecyparis obtusa 'Crippsii' (golden yellow)

Chamaecyparis pisifera 'Boulevard' (dense silvery)

Juniperus x media 'Blaauw' (deep blueish-green)

COLUMNAR

Chamaecyparis lawsoniana 'Columnaris' (dense bluish-green)

Cupressus macrocarpa 'Donard Gold' (golden-yellow)

Platycladus orientalis 'Elegantissima' (bright green turning bronze in winter)

Platycladus orientalis 'Golden Rocket' (bright green turning bronze in winter)

SPREADING

Juniperus conferta 'Blue Pacific' (dense blue-green)

J. horizontalis 'Wiltonii' (blue-green turning purple in winter)

J. x media 'Gold Coast' (golden tips)

Protect a young hedge with a windbreak of nylon netting which is taller than the tallest plant.

Clip hedging plants in their formative years to ensure healthy growth.

HEDGING SHRUBS

Abelia spp.	Dovyalis caffra (Kei apple)
Barleria obtusa (bush violet)	Hibiscus rosa-sinensis
Bougainvilleas	Lonicera nitida 'Baggesen's Gold'
Carissa macrocarpa	(box honeysuckle)
C. 'Green Carpet' (Natal plum)	Plumbago auriculata (blue plumbago)
Cotoneaster spp.	Rhododendron spp. (azaleas)
Cupressocyparus leylandii	Roses
Clerodendron spp.	Spiraea cantoniensis (Cape May)

HEDGES

The first necessity for any flourishing hedge is to give it a good start by digging a trench 50 cm deep and 50 cm wide and filling it with top soil, compost and superphosphate, well mixed. Water this well to settle it, top it up with compost if necessary, then plant the hedging plants.

The general rule for spacing is that those hedge subjects which will grow to approximately a metre or so in height should be planted 30 cm apart, while those which will grow much taller can be placed at one metre intervals.

While your hedge is small, you can protect it with a windbreak of nylon netting. The eventual height of the hedge should be taken into account, how rampant a grower it is and whether the plants chosen are suitable for a formally clipped hedge or a more informal, rambling hedge. Bear in mind that the roots of some hedges are likely to invade the neighbouring soil.

The second necessity for good hedge growth is to clip hedging plants sufficiently in their first few, formative years. When trimming a grown hedge, aim for a neat effect, with sides either upright or preferably sloping inwards (never outwards) at the top (*see* illustration on page 162).

Flowering hedging plants should be kept clipped until the season before they are due to bloom. For instance azaleas can be clipped until late autumn or early winter, then allowed to develop their buds into flowers. After flowering, clipping can be resumed. Bougainvillea hedges can be clipped back as hard as is necessary immediately after flowering, and given an extra feed to produce new leaves. Then, when the first signs of buds appear, cut back on water and food to encourage them to produce a good crop of flowers.

Climbing plants

Climbers will cover an unsightly building, clothe a boring wall, tumble gracefully over an arch or find their way up a pergola to spread a lovely, natural 'shade cloth'. You can even use them to create a quick vertical screen of growth to conceal an unwanted view or gain badly needed privacy.

Apart from all these uses, some climbing plants will obligingly serve as ground covers. Think of ivy, which will make a cool, dark-green carpet under a large tree, or star jasmine (*Trachelospermum jasminoides*) which will spread in the dappled shade of lightly leafed trees such as silver birches. Some climbers are even capable of creating good sturdy hedges if trained for this purpose.

Climbers may be deciduous or evergreen. An evergreen climber will bring permanent shade to the patio, whereas a deciduous one will let the sun through in winter. There are many options when choosing a creeper for your garden. Assess your needs and explore the possibilities.

LEFT *A clematis has climbed from the cool damp earth to put on show its truly magnificent cascade of beautiful flowers, and accompanied by two perfect pink roses. Clematis hybrids can be cut back almost to the ground in autumn. Propagate them by laying small sections of stem horizontally in clean sand, or by planting seeds.*

BELOW *Ivy* (Hedera helix) *clings close to the wall to create a living cover surrounding the window box of lobelias and pansies.*

OPPOSITE PAGE RIGHT Hibiscus rosa-sinensis *has been hybridized into what is surely among the most glamorous of garden shrubs. Like most hybrids, 'Volcano', pictured here, will not take frost but will grow readily in containers which can be covered or brought indoors in winter. If the leaves wilt, cut back the stem until you find the stem borer, and destroy it.*

OPPOSITE PAGE LEFT *Regimented and neatly clipped lines of laurel* (Laurus nobilis), Westringia fruticosa *and boxwood* (Buxus sempervirens), *lend an air of formality to a terraced garden. Regular clipping will keep these plants in good shape.*

CHOICE OF SUPPORT

As its immediate task is to climb, your climber must be given support by means of strong twine, wire or, initially, slender sticks, to lead it up to the wall or other main support.

Your choice of support depends on the extent and weight of the climber when fully grown. (Enquire about this at your garden centre when you buy your plant.) Climbers like honeysuckle or clematis which do not literally stick themselves on, can be grown against a wall or fence but will need trellis or straining wire. Screw vertical sections of wood batten to the wall with sizeable screws in wall plugs and hammer the trellis on with galvanized nails. Straining wire – stretched through wire 'eyes' in vertical, horizontal, diagonal or even diamond shapes – should be strong and galvanized. Strong wire netting can also be used. Special nails, plastic ties and clips are available to secure stems.

Vigorous rambling roses, wisterias, bougainvilleas and the trumpet creeper (Campsis radicans) will need a stronger support like a pergola or an arch. Light annual climbers can be grown on plastic netting or lighter wire. Special preformed trellis is available, in arch or fan shapes, ready to fix on to a wall.

Freestanding metal arches are on sale at garden centres and a handy carpenter can build you a romantic rustic wooden one to carry that glorious

RIGHT *An ordinary garden room has taken on an air of mystery and charm by the addition of a roof of ivy* (Hedera helix)*. A small-leafed ivy nearby has added its own quota of soft, soothing green.*

WAYS OF CLIMBING

Some climbing plants are self-supporting, using tendrils and leaf stalks to cling to the supporting wire or trellis. Others, for example the Virginia creeper (Parthenocissus quinquefolia), has tiny pads which it spreads over the host wall or fence. Ivy (Hedera spp.) too, will cling close. Others, such as jasmine, twist and twine. Aerial rootlets help plants such as the delicious monster (Monstera deliciosa) and the trumpet vine (Clytostoma callistegioides) to cling on to surfaces tenaciously.

Then there are the climbing roses and bougainvilleas, producing long, sturdy stems which have to be trained, right from the start. Their thorns help them clamber and hook on to any willing support.

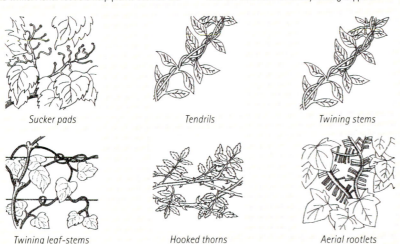

Sucker pads

Tendrils

Twining stems

Twining leaf-stems

Hooked thorns

Aerial rootlets

TRAINING

Training must start straight away, by taking side shoots and leading them along horizontal lines. Pinching out terminal growth will encourage more shoots to develop.

Those climbers without twining stems, leaf stems or tendrils, will have to be tied in. Do so regularly so that the plant spreads evenly.

Ensure that you leave enough space in your loop or clip for expansion of the stem or side shoot. Tie shoots in horizontally, not vertically, where at all possible. With some climbers, more flowers are produced on horizontal shoots.

Climbing rose stems can actually be twined around uprights while they are still young and pliable. The young rose stems can also be tied on to a wire shape.

climbing rose. Do ensure that the feet of your arch are firmly fixed into cement. Wooden uprights are first fixed on to metal T-shapes and these are placed in the cement. Don't mulch too close to a wooden upright, to keep it as dry as possible and avoid rotting. Make sure the wood is treated with a plant-friendly preservative.

Arches make wonderful focal points or frames. Place one across a path, behind a small bench, over a garden gate or even the front door, or at the top of a few steps between garden levels.

CARE AND MAINTENANCE

Those climbers such as Virginia creeper and ivy, which cling on with small pads and roots, will leave these behind if ever they are taken down. To avoid having to scrub or scrape them off, it is wise to attach wire netting firmly to the wall for the plant to climb. Then just peel off the netting to remove the creeper. This method is also useful for reasonably light climbers which do not leave behind pads or roots, but grow against a wall which periodically needs to be painted. If the netting is carefully eased

BELOW Planted at the top of the wall, among the crotons (Codiaeum spp.) and palms, bougainvilleas and golden shower (Pyrostegia venusta) have obligingly cascaded down the wall, to create a glorious exuberance of living colour.

BELOW Allamanda cathartica *has substantial leaves and trumpets of gleaming yellow. A warm climate subject, it can be persuaded to climb over an arch or along a fence, or to cascade over a low wall.*

forward, maintenance can be done without sacrificing the lovely covering of leaves and flowers.

Roots of climbers can become most invasive and they should not be planted close to drains. The tickey creeper (*Ficus pumila*) has been known to block up nearby drains completely. If a climber has relatively slender growth, this does not mean that its roots are similarly slender.

Some climbers, such as the pink dipladenia (*Mandevilla splendens*), need good circulation of air around them and will not grow close to a wall. While it is better to grow them over an open fence or arch, if you have to place them against a wall leave a space of at least 30 cm between the supporting trellis or frame and the wall.

Some climbers do well in containers, so it is possible to place them on a paved patio without digging a hole. Think of the many clematis hybrids and cultivars, the wax plant (*Hoya carnosa*) and even the bougainvilleas and annual climbers such as black-eyed Susan (*Thunbergia alata*).

A flowering creeper which has been allowed to climb up through a tree can look spectacular. A deciduous tree with a bougainvillea entwined in it is a lovely sight. But give careful thought to the relative weights of tree and creeper. The extra weight could cause the top-heavy tree to swing dangerously in the wind or even collapse.

You can also try planting a stout pole and allowing a creeper to climb over it.

Bougainvilleas must be cut back hard after the flowering period. Then give them plenty of food and water to encourage new growth. Cut water right down as soon as new buds appear.

Chewing gum and Prestik will hold stems of delicate climbers in place.

CLIMBING PLANTS

ANNUAL CLIMBERS

Cobaea scandens (cup-and-saucer vine)
Cucumis sativus (cucumber)
Lathyrus odoratus (sweet pea)
Phaseolus vulgaris (beans)
Thunbergia alata (black-eyed Susan)
Tropaeolum majus (nasturtium)

FLOWERING CLIMBERS

Allamanda cathartica (golden trumpet-vine)
Antigonon leptopus (coral vine)
Beaumontia grandiflora (Nepal trumpet climber)
Bougainvillea hybrids
Campsis radicans (trumpet vine)

Clematis hybrids
Distictis buccinatoria (Mexican trumpet, previously *Bignonia cherere*)
Gelsemium sempervirens (Carolina yellow jasmine)
Jasminum polyanthum (Chinese jasmine)
Lonicera spp. (honeysuckle)
Mandevilla laxa (Chilean jasmine)
Mandevilla splendens (pink dipladenia)
Maurandia barclaiana (creeping gloxinia)
Pandorea jasminoides (bower plant)
Petrea volubilis (purple wreath)
Pyrostegia venusta (golden shower)
Rosa spp. (roses)
Senecio tamoides (canary creeper)

Solanum jasminoides (potato vine)
Solanum wendlandii (potato creeper)
Stephanotis floribunda (Madagascar jasmine)
Strongylodon macrobotrys (jade vine)
Thunbergia grandiflora (blue trumpet vine)
Trachelospermum jasminoides (star jasmine)
Wisteria spp.

FOLIAGE CLIMBERS

Hedera spp. (ivy)
Monstera deliciosa (delicious monster)
Parthenocissus quinquefolia (Virginia creeper)
Philodendron spp.
Vitis vinifera (grape vine)

Position

Shade or sun? This is an important factor when positioning shrubs and climbers. Morning sun suits very nearly all shrubs, but the hot afternoon sun can cause great distress. Many plants will be happy under filtered shade from sparsely leaved trees, but will find dense shade disturbing. Most plants with coloured leaves are at their best in full sun, as their colour is likely to fade in deep shade.

To give them a good start, plant shrubs in the same way as trees (see page 36) but adjust the size of the hole.

How to plant a shrub

Well-drained soil is essential for very nearly all plants. Roots that are allowed to become water-logged will surely die and so will the plant. Make a square hole at least twice the size of the root ball. Keep back the top soil and mix this with bonemeal, superphosphate and compost. Some plants have feeding roots near the soil's surface, so a plant should never be placed any deeper than it was in the container. Follow the same method as for tree-planting as regards level, backfilling and firming (see

page 36). Water well and stake if necessary. A permanent mulch around your newly planted shrub will keep the soil cool and the plant fed. Fertilizer such as 2:3:2 should only be given once the plant is well established. Never plant a climber closer than 30 cm from the wall or other support, or the soil may be too hot or in the rain shadow of the support.

LEFT Clematis *hybrids present their gorgeous open-faced flowers in spring. They will hapily grow in the sun or semi-shade, but like to have their roots cool, damp and well fed. Plant them at least 15 cm lower than in their original container.*

BELOW Acer palmatum *'Bloodgood' boasts spring leaves with a pink tinge. They turn to burgundy lasting through into autumn. With its rounded shape and richly coloured leaves it can be used as a specimen. It will also look splendid with smaller shrubs or brightly coloured annuals and perennials.*

SMALL SHRUBS

Allamanda neriifolia (golden trumpet)
Berberis x media 'Park Juwel' (barberry)
B. thunbergii 'Atropurpurea Nana'
Callistemon viminalis 'Captain Cook' (bottlebrush)
C. viminalis 'Little John' (dwarf bottlebrush)
Cistus x hybrids (rock rose)
Coleonema spp. (confetti bush)
Hebe spp. (Veronicas)
Heliotropium arborescens (heliotrope)
Ixora spp. (flame of the woods)
Justicia brandegeana (shrimp flower)
Leptospermum scoparium 'Cherry Brandy' (tea bush)
Mandevilla sanderi (shrub dipladenia)
Pentas lanceolata (star cluster)
Reinwardtia trigyna (yellow flax)
Ruellia macrantha (Christmas pride)
Spiraea x arguta (bridal wreath)
S. japonica 'Anthony Waterer' (pink may)

Lawns

An attractive sweep of smooth, green grass is a wonderful asset to any garden and can make up for a scarcity of flowers, while a badly kept lawn will certainly detract from your beautiful beds. But a good lawn requires preparation and a practically year-round programme of care.

Size and shape

Nowhere in the garden are plants closer together than they are in the lawn. In fact, the closer they are, the better the lawn.

But this also means that those close-packed roots are continually taking goodness from the soil to the leaves which are then cut back and the grass is driven to create new growth, thus demanding more nutrition and water.

Give careful thought to the size and site of your lawn. Make a lawn of a size you can cope with and give the rest of the garden over to shrubs and perennials. In very shady spots such as under large trees or close to the south side of buildings, plant Shade-Over or Kearsney grass, bearing in mind that Kearsney cannot take heavy frost.

The high traffic in some oft-trodden routes will damage grass, breaking it down and compacting the soil, so use paving here or stepping-stones attractively interplanted with a small, tough ground cover.

A square lawn will be fairly easy to mow, as will gentle curves that are not too sharp. Bear this in mind when planting your lawn. A steep slope will make mowing difficult, but don't avoid gentle slopes as these can be attractive.

Small beds sprinkled about the lawn can look bitty. It is also more difficult to mow around them and to keep their edges looking tidy. As small beds break up the sweep of the lawn, they also tend to make it look smaller. A large expanse of lawn is elegant and lovely.

Levelling and preparation

Even on a slope, the soil's surface should be even. If the slope is long and steep, why not consider one or two lawned terraces, with walls between? To achieve an even surface, remove bumps and fill in hollows, breaking up any lumps and taking out any stones in the top 20 cm of soil. Dig the soil over and rake it. Judge your levels by driving wooden pegs into the soil at intervals and laying a straight edge (a piece of flat wood or metal which you have already established is quite straight) and a spirit level across them. This is not as tedious as it sounds and will save a great deal of trouble later on. If there is a great deal of levelling to be done, then the topsoil should be put to one side and replaced when levelling is over.

To prepare the soil for planting, dig it over to a depth of at least 20 cm, incorporating compost. Adding sand and compost improves heavy clay soil and adding plenty of compost to sandy soil enriches it and improves water retention. Then level the area again and apply a general fertilizer such as 2:3:2 — about 100 g (a handful) per square metre. The effort you put into preparation will ultimately determine the success of your lawn.

At this stage, a multitude of weeds may find conditions very much to their liking and it is a good idea to allow them to come up, once or twice, and rake them out or treat them with the correct, non-residual herbicide, before planting your lawn. Obtain advice about herbicides from your garden centre or lawn specialist.

ABOVE *Kearsney grass has broad blades and makes a thick, green cover. Its main advantage is that it will grow in the shade. Unfortunately it cannot take heavy frost.*

OPPOSITE PAGE *A lawn in perfect condition, weed-free, emerald green and healthy, is an important asset to the garden and sets off the flowers to perfection. The flowers have been allowed to spill over on to the grass to good effect, and should be gently pushed back out of the way for mowing.*

RUNNERS

Each runner has three or four nodes. Some leaves are left visible above ground. Firm them in and keep moist until the grass is established.

to eight weeks throughout the season. Always accompany fertilizer with generous watering so as not to burn the grass. You can also apply a slow-release fertilizer and water the lawn later.

PLUGS

Trays generally contain 200 small plants, each with a well-established root system and leaves. This number will on average cover eight square metres. Insert the plants about 20 cm apart (closer if you are trying to get your lawn going in a hurry), firming the soil around each one. Water every day for 10 days, then every fourth day for a fortnight, thereafter one thorough weekly soaking will be sufficient. Fertilize as for runners.

ABOVE A well-kept lawn is a joy to behold and is sheer pleasure to walk on. A maintenance programme of feeding, watering and mowing, starting in early spring, is essential to keep that green sward looking its best.

Planting a new lawn

With the exception of the really cold months in frost-prone inland areas, you can establish a lawn at any time of year provided you have a water supply sufficient for irrigation. Where laid-on water is limited, plant only during the rainy season. Generally spring to late summer or autumn planting will give best results.

There are four major planting methods.

RUNNERS

Runners are obtainable in bags from garden centres. Prepare furrows about 20 cm apart and 6 cm deep, placing furrows across, not up and down, a slope. Plant the runners in the furrows and firm them in. Each runner should have at least three or four nodes and some of the grass leaves should be left visible above ground. Smooth the soil slightly and water well. Ensure that the whole area is kept well watered until the grass is established. Alternate a general fertilizer and a high-nitrogen one every six

RIGHT Plugs of grass make lawn planting easy. Each plug is well developed and has been grown in a fertile medium which means it will be self-sustaining as it settles into its new environment.

SEED

Read the package instructions for quantity of seed per metre and follow this carefully. Make a series of shallow furrows about 15 cm apart, scatter the seed evenly, then rake across the surface to ensure even distribution. Seed sown on slopes may have to be covered with pegged-down shadecloth or sacking to prevent its being washed away. Remove the cover once the seeds sprout. Don't water before sowing, but give a good, gentle and thorough soaking after sowing. Water frequently thereafter, only reducing when the seedlings are about 2 cm high. Then, in stages, reduce watering to about once a week. Do not mow too soon. Mow first when the grass is about 10 cm high and then only cut off the top one or two centimetres. Fertilize as for runners.

TURF OR INSTANT LAWN

Although this is the most expensive way of making a new lawn, it is also very convenient and quick and is especially useful for slopes. Preparation of the soil is just as important as for other methods, and after planting, heavy watering is essential to penetrate the thick growth. The supply and laying of turf is normally carried out by specialist growers, who will advise on the kind of grass (choice is usually limited) and prepare the soil for planting. Do choose a reputable supplier so that you do not import a lifetime's supply of persistent weeds.

Do not mow until the grass is about 5 cm high and do not cut it too short for some weeks. If the edges of the sections of turf become visible, the soil in between may have been washed down with watering. Fill in the gaps with light soil, gently brushed in. Once the grass is well-established, continue with a programme of fertilizing as for runners.

Renovation and maintenance

Neglected lawns end up with compacted soil and, with some grasses, a thick thatch which prevents nutrients, water and air reaching the soil. Generally most lawns should be given special treatment around August to spruce them up and prepare them for the growing season.

Cut the lawn low enough for the stem runners to be visible and remove the clippings. Then scarify it with a wire rake to loosen any over-long and dead runners and sweep these away with a sturdy broom. Kikuyu in particular needs this treatment, but be a little gentler with the finer grasses. Then with a spiked roller, a hollow tined fork or any garden fork, spike the lawn all over, about 10 cm into the soil, to aerate it. Don't forget slopes, which may not look compacted, but which need especial help in getting water, which might otherwise run off, down to the winter-weary grass roots. After scarifying and spiking, give the whole lawn a good soaking, apply fertilizer, then water again.

The following is the generally accepted programme for fertilizing a lawn. In spring apply a general fertilizer such as 2:3:2 or 2:3:4 to establish a good root system and healthy foliage. Water this in thoroughly. Thereafter, apply a high-nitrogen fertilizer

BELOW A neat edge to the lawn will separate flowers and grass. Cut down into the grass with a long, sharp knife or spade, but take care to keep to the same line. This will prevent the formation of a deep, steep 'cliff' at the lawn's edge.

like 4:1:1, LAN or ammonium sulphate every six to eight weeks to keep the foliage green and healthy. Alternate the two kinds of fertilizer throughout the season. Use either an applicator on the hose, or apply granules with a spreader or by hand.

To ensure an even sprinkling, use string to divide the lawn into strips or squares. Always water thoroughly after fertilizing.

Top-dressing is not essential, but is useful to even out bumps or after very rigorous aeration. Obtain a good top-dressing (light loam) from a reputable supplier or again you could end up with a tiresome invasion of new kinds of weeds.

In April, to help the lawn withstand winter, carry out the spring-cleaning process again.

Watering

Watering should always be deep, as shallow watering encourages roots to grow too near the surface. In the summer-rainfall areas, the first rains will probably bring the lawn into good growth. It is important to check on just how much water is getting down into the soil. Dig down, and make sure it is going down at least 10 cm. If you have an average kind of soil, water once or twice a week in summer and less often in spring and autumn.

Do not water certain local grasses in winter as they should remain dormant then.

Mowing and edging

Mow often to stimulate the growth of the lawn, cutting off the same amount each time. It is usual to keep coarse grasses 3 – 4 cm and finer grasses 2 cm high. Grass in the shade is kept longer than that in the sun. The rate of growth, which varies according to the season, will determine the frequency of mowing. Kikuyu probably needs mowing once or twice a week year-round, except winter, while some other grasses need less mowing both at the height of summer and in winter. Remove clippings and place them on your compost heap.

Don't mow the lawn when it is wet. Mowing cross-wise to the previous time you mowed achieves an even surface over time.

If you want some paving in your lawn, make sure you lay it 1 – 2 cm below the lawn, so that your mower is not damaged.

Keeping the edges of a lawn neat is probably the most time-consuming of tasks. Nylon-line trimmers, electric or petrol-driven, are useful. If you are unused to operating one, practise on an open field first, as clumsy handling could destroy garden plants. If you do not have a power trimmer, cut down carefully around the beds with a spade.

To prevent grasses invading beds, lay down a mower strip or embed a corrugated metal or plastic strip between grass and bed.

RIGHT *Wonderlawn – with its small, round, dark-green leaves forming a dense mat – makes an attractive lawn in shady, low-traffic areas. It should be carefully controlled as it can take over. Where shade is very heavy its growth tends to become straggly.*

VARIETIES OF GRASS

There are grasses to suit both every part of the garden – from sun to shade – and different parts of the country. Some have local names, such as Harrismith, Berea and Florida, and the specialist lawn growers have developed varieties and mixes for all conditions. It is difficult to say conclusively which grass is best for a specific area, so in your particular area it is best to consult your local garden centres or one of the major lawn suppliers. Here is a limited list of grasses to give you some background before you consult your garden centre.

BUFFALO

This has fairly broad leaves and is suited to coastal areas. It will not withstand frost, but will grow in semi-shade.

BEREA

A broad-leafed grass also suited to warmer parts. It is frost-sensitive and prefers sun, but will grow fairly well in semi-shade.

KEARSNEY

This broad-leafed grass is highly suited to warm regions where it will also grow in shady areas.

SILVERTON BLUE

A slow-growing grass with an attractive dark bluish-green hue and fine leaves. It is hardy and once established needs little mowing. Can take some shade.

FLORIDA

This is one of the best-known fine grasses, particularly on the Highveld. It makes lawns with a fine texture and a good mat, but needs plenty of feeding and watering.

BAYVIEW

One of the more popular varieties, this has fine leaves and is tolerant of frost.

KIKUYU

This is often praised as the best lawn grass, while some gardeners regard it as an absolute scourge. There is no doubt that a well-maintained kikuyu lawn can look green and lush, but it does demand constant attention. It has earned a bad reputation for its tendency to invade adjacent flower beds and paths. It needs regular fertilizing and watering and a heavy-duty mower must be used or it will form too thick a mat and over-coarse leaves. Well kept, a kikuyu lawn can be a fine sight.

LMG (LOW MAINTENANCE GRASS)

This is slow-growing and frost-hardy, has fine leaves and needs little mowing.

HARRISMITH

This grass makes a fine-leafed lawn. It will tolerate heavy frost, but will not grow well in the shade.

ROYAL CAPE

This is as popular in the Cape as Florida is on the Highveld. It has a fine texture and is not very resistant to drought.

GULF GREEN

This recent introduction is recommended for its tolerance of drought and frost, its vigorous growth and fine leaves.

SKAAPPLAAS

Another fine grass, this will grow in warm or cool gardens, spreading quickly to form a dense mat which will need plenty of water during summer.

SHADE-OVER

This is a blend of grasses adapted to shade conditions. If mown at the correct height it will thrive for many years, but it will not tolerate low mowing.

ALL SEASONS EVERGREEN

This is a cool season grass not suitable for sub-tropical areas, which needs copious watering during the summer months. It has the great advantage of being bright green through autumn and winter, when other grasses have died down.

OTHER COVERS

Wonderlawn's small, round, dark-green leaves form a dense mat which makes an attractive lawn in shady, low-traffic areas. It can take over and where shade is very heavy, its growth becomes straggly. Daisy lawn *(Phyla nodiflora)* has tough foliage and bears a mass of daisies close to the ground.

Perennials

The word *perennial* covers a wide spectrum of plants, from the lowest groundcover to tall cannas and verbascums. It includes all those plants which endure through the years, some dying down in winter, others keeping their leaves throughout the year. Perennials have the reputation of being able to look after themselves, so we are inclined to neglect them, leaving them to their own devices year after year. Pay them a little extra attention and it will work wonders.

Lasting & self-multiplying

Among perennials you will find bulbs, rhizomes, tubers and corms; herbaceous plants (multistemmed plants such as Michaelmas daisies) and evergreens such as agapanthus. Perennials come into their own in the mixed border, where they grow, bloom and multiply, but they need to be divided every few years in spring or autumn. When the clumps are divided, the outer, vigorous growth should be separated off and planted out, and the inner, older, worn-out growth discarded. (See pages 164 – 165 for information on how to divide the various kinds of perennials.)

If certain perennials take on an untidy look at times, the clumps can be lifted and placed in an out-of-the-way spot in the garden where, kept just damp, they can stay until it is time to divide them and plant them out ready for the next season. Some perennials, such as agapanthus and watsonias, take time to settle down after division and will not bloom the first season or two thereafter.

Bulbs

This commonly used gardening term includes true bulbs (such as liliums and daffodils), rhizomes (bearded irises and cannas), corms (gladioli, watsonias), and tubers (dahlias, tuberous begonias). All have the ability to store food and they remain living entities year-round. Even when they are dormant and apparently dead they are nevertheless alive.

The two main flowering periods for bulbs are spring and summer, and planting times are autumn and early spring. Bulbs are a wonderful investment in beauty and a yearly source of delight, as those seemingly lifeless brown shapes grow in rich, damp soil, to produce a lavish display of colourful blooms.

Some bulbs are excellent in containers. See planting details and combinations on page 93.

WINTER AND SPRING BULBS

These bring glorious colour to the garden as the cold months draw to an end.

Planting

Even as early as February, garden centres start selling those brilliantly coloured packets depicting exquisite ranunculi, daffodils, anemones and many others. It is probably a good idea to buy them before they are sold out, but don't plant them yet. Keep them in a cool place, the best being the vegetable tray in the fridge. The best time for planting most of these bulbs is in April, when the soil is cooling down. Treated tulips are usually only available in May, when they are planted.

Most winter and spring bulbs like to be in the sun for most of the day, but will grow where they receive morning sun and afternoon shade. Their soil should be as well-drained as possible. If you are doubtful about the efficiency of drainage, rather plant your bulbs in containers or half-fill every

ABOVE *Tall and splendid Neomarica caerulea, a member of the iris family, can never be ignored. A well-establilshed plant will produce dozens of purple blooms with brown-striped centres throughout the season from spring into autumn. Well-drained soil in the sun or semi shade, with either liquid manure or a general fertilizer every three or four weeks and regular watering will encourage it to put on its exhibition of beautiful blooms.*

OPPOSITE PAGE *All the exuberance of summer is to be seen in this mixed border. Low-growing white agapanthus, day lilies of many shades, a tall and elegant verbascum, Inca lilies and poppy seedheads have come together in a glorious summer profusion.*

RIGHT *Hellebores bloom in the winter and early spring garden, producing unusual flowers of white pink or purple, or with a touch of green. They grow well in the shade or semi-shade, but never where the afternoon sun can burn them. Give them organically enriched soil, and frequent waterings during summer.*

BELOW *A group of tulips in bounding good health brings with it an air of luxury. Treated tulips are planted in May into soil enriched with compost, with a dessertspoon of bonemeal and one of superhosphate mixed into the soil of each hole. They will be most unhappy in extreme heat, and even the glare from a nearby white wall could upset them.*

planting hole in your garden bed with cinders or gravel. Dig the soil well to loosen it, and add plenty of well-matured compost. If you are using kraal manure, this must be completely rotted. If it is not and it comes into contact with the bulbs, the bulbs themselves will surely rot. Probably the safest method is to place the bulbs on a layer of sand.

Both bonemeal, which is slowly released into the soil, and superphosphate will help produce healthy growth. Add these at planting time, 25 g of superphosphate sprinkled over each square metre of soil, and a small handful of bonemeal mixed into the hole for each bulb.

Depth of planting differs for each kind of bulb, but a good general rule is to plant a bulb to at least three times its depth. Some of the exceptions are ifafa lilies, crinums and *Amaryllis hippeastrum*, which should have about the top half of the bulb above ground level.

Dig the hole, place the bulb in the bottom, preferably on a bed of sand, and add a small handful of bonemeal to the filling soil before replacing it. Mark the spot where the bulbs are planted. If bulbs and annuals are to be mixed, it is best to plant the seedlings first, then the bulbs, as otherwise the bulbs may be damaged as you dig in for the seedlings.

On-going care

Once planted, bulbs should never be allowed to dry out. Keep the soil damp at all times. As soon as growth is well under way a good soaking should be given once a week, rather than frequent surface sprinklings which will encourage the roots to come up and be burnt by the heat of the sun. A layer of mulch will not only keep the soil cool, but also keep the plants well fed.

The bulb will send out roots in search of food and water, and leaves will find their way up to the sunshine above. Once the leaves are growing well, the plants can be given either a sprinkling of general fertilizer or an application of weak liquid seaweed manure every ten days.

A wealth of choice

When you are planning your winter and spring bulb planting, it is worth knowing that many are obtainable packed as single colours, not mixed. Dutch irises may be deep or pale blue, deep or pale yellow, as well as white. Ranunculi and tulips come in a wider and brilliant range, also packed as individual colours.

Good mixers in your flower bed include tall Dutch irises underplanted with lobelias, alyssum or muscari (grape hyacinth) or mixed with anemones and ranunculi. Daffodils look good in the company of pansies, violas, lobelia, alyssum or nemophila.

Daffodils are surely the best-loved spring bulbs. They make a splendid impact when planted in groups rather than sprinklings of one or two. To create a gloriously natural scene under a spreading tree which is still bare of leaves in late winter, dig the soil over well and plant a mass of daffodil bulbs. Then sow the seed of Italian rye grass. Keep the area well watered, and the grass will come up with the bulbs. Once blooming is over, the daffodils' leaves can be allowed to die down, then both grass and leaves can be cut down to the ground as the tree's new leaves cast their shadows.

The paperwhite daffodil is prized for its ability to send up tall leaves and stems bearing white flowers, even from a bed of gravel.

Tulips should not be planted before May. If you only buy them then, it is imperative that you get cold-treated tulips which must be planted immediately. Otherwise, buy your untreated tulip bulbs in February or March, and keep them in the fridge until mid- or late May. Enjoying enormous popularity of late are clivias, our beautiful indigenous flames of the

BULBS & PERENNIALS

WINTER & SPRING PERENNIALS/BULBS

Allium neapolitanum (florist allium)
Alstroemeria aurea (Inca lily)
Bulbinella robusta (cat's tail)
Diascia integerrima (twinspur)
Gazania spp.
Heuchera sanguinea (coral bells)
Iris spp.
Nierembergia repens (cup flower)
Papaver orientale (oriental poppy)
Penstemon hybrids
Scabiosa spp. (scabious)
Veltheimia bracteata (forest lily)
Zantedeschia aethiopica (arum lily)

OTHER PERENNIALS

Anemone coronaria (garden anemone)
Arctotis spp. (African daisy)
Astilbe x arendsii (goat's beard)
Campanula spp. (bell flower)
Babiana stricta (babiana)
Bergenia cordifolia (heartleaf bergenia)
Cerastium tomentosum (snow-in-summer)

Clivia miniata (bush lily/flame of the forest)
Cyrtanthus mackenii (ifafa lily)
Drosanthemum speciosum (vygie)
Euryops pectinatus (grey-leafed euryops)
Freesia hybrids (freesia)
Gazania spp.
Gladiolus hybrids
Hyacinthus orientalis (hyacinth)
Iris spp.
Ixia hybrids (wand flower)
Lachenalia spp. (Cape cowslip)
Leucojum aestivum (snowflake)
Muscari armeniacum (grape hyacinth)
Narcissus spp. (daffodil, narcissus)
Nerine spp.
Nierembergia spp. (cup flower)
Osteospermum ecklonis (Van Staden's
    River daisy)
Sparaxis hybrids (harlequin flower)
Tritonia hybrids (blazing star)
Tulipa hybrids (tulip)
Viola odorata (violet)
Watsonia spp. (watsonia)

LEFT *Louisiana irises are known as water irises or bog irises but while they like to have their feet in water, they will happily grow in the main garden where soil is heavily enriched with organics. They need plenty of water to keep the heavy growth of foliage healthy. Louisiana irises should be planted at least 10 cm down into the soil, as opposed to bearded irises which are planted almost on the soil's surface.*

OPPOSITE PAGE Dahlia imperialis grows to three metres, demanding little attention but producing a mass of single mauve flowers high up above the main garden.

forest, whose hybrids are much sought after. In their natural environment they grow on the forest floor, where they thrive thanks to shade and good drainage through layers of rotted leaves. They can be left undisturbed for many years, lighting their shady corner with their large heads of tubular flowers. With the right care they also make excellent container plants.

Irises come in many lovely shapes and forms. Bearded irises bloom in spring, growing from rhizomes which should sit on the surface with their roots reaching down into the soil. To divide them, cut the rhizomes cleanly through, ensuring that each section is left with an eye on it.

Other spring bloomers are the Dutch irises, their stems tall and slender. Louisiana irises love to be near water, but will grow elsewhere if they are given copious quantities of water during the spring growing and blooming season. Their rhizomes should be planted to a depth of about 7,5 cm.

Kaempferi irises come into bloom in early summer, sporting wide floppy petals in a variety of shades. They will grow in or near water and need to be given regular feeds of liquid manure or general fertilizer from early spring.

Favourite South African winter and spring bulbs include freesias, babianas, ixias, lachenalia, ornithogalum (chincherinchees), sparaxis, tritonia and watsonias, many of which have been hybridized.

SUMMER BULBS

These rest during the cold months, then come to life in spring and bring forth their flowers in summer, many of them making bold splashes of colour.

Dahlias, liliums and cannas are probably the most spectacular, but there are many others, including agapanthus of several sizes, *Kniphofias* (red-hot pokers), highly coloured *Hemerocallis* hybrids (day lilies) and tuberous begonias for garden and containers.

From the dramatic blooms of the March lily *(Amaryllis belladonna)*, gladiolus, schizostylis, watsonias and the summer-flowering arums *(Zantedeschia spp.)* to the more delicate charm of *Dietes grandiflora*, nerine and *Tulbaghia simmleri* (sweet garlic) and the quaint beauty of *Eucomis* and *Sandersonia spp.*, there is a wealth of summer bulbs to choose from. Planting methods are the same as for winter and spring bulbs and all are indigenous sun lovers.

Other popular perennials

Herbaceous perennials are those which send up stems in spring to bear leaves, flowers and eventually seeds. They then die down completely in winter. For complete dormancy they require a cold winter, but some will grow where winters are only mild. These include the Michaelmas daisies *(Aster novi-belgii)*, achilleas, physostegias and chrysanthemums. They are all good mixers and should be divided in autumn or spring.

RIGHT Lilium 'Stargazer' is a summer bloomer of exquisite beauty. Bulbs should be planted to about three times the depth of the bulb, with a handful of bonemeal being mixed into the soil at the bottom of the hole. Place the bulb on to a bed of sand and mark the spot. Although lilium bulbs like to be kept damp during their growing season, they should never be allowed to become waterlogged.

PLANTING AND PROPAGATION TIPS

- Lilium bulbs – plump and free of any disease – should be planted as soon after purchase as possible.
- When dividing dahlia clumps, each tuber must have a piece of the mother stem with it.
- When removing a flowered stem from a canna, give it a sharp tug to remove the whole thing, so that the healthy adjoining stem can grow and bloom.
- Alstroemeria's flowered stems should also be pulled out completely.
- In spring chrysanthemums and dahlias will send up succulent new shoots from a seemingly dead clump. These can be cut cleanly through, and planted out as cuttings, which will grow into healthy new plants.

Acanthus mollis (wild rhubarb), whose attractive leaves were immortalized by Greek sculptors, will grow in semi-shade and shade. It likes a rich soil and plenty of water from early spring. *Anemone hupehensis*, the lovely Japanese or wind anemone, bears flowers of pinkish mauve or white on tall, slender stems during February and March. It likes a cool root run and will grow in sun, semi-shade or full shade. Achillea or yarrow will survive in poor soil, but insists on good drainage in full sun. It can spread alarmingly, so take care to keep it in check. The 'Turkish Delight' series has prettily coloured flowers of yellow and shades of pink.

Astilbe cultivars send up slender stems of feathery leaves and have dainty plumes of flower heads in pink, white or mauve. They are ideal for the edge of a pond, as they need plenty of water during spring and summer, and even in winter when they are dormant they should not be allowed to dry out completely. Bergamot or monarda, which spreads its roots fast, bears spidery heads of flowers on slender stems in summer.

Chrysanthemums are surely among the best of autumn flowers, with their spicy, aromatic scent. They should be divided often. Many gardeners like to cut their chrysanthemum stems down to half their height in mid-December, to promote better blooming in autumn. In spring the new shoots which arise from the clump can be cleanly cut away and planted as cuttings.

Michaelmas daisies range from tall to short and have a colour range from white through pinks to mauve and purple. They are most obliging plants and are not fussy about soil as long as they have a well-drained, sunny position. They must be divided often.

Penstemons die down in winter, then come up to join the other members of the spring and summer garden, carrying masses of bell-like flowers up their stems. *Phlox paniculata*, the perennial phlox, is a summer bloomer with tall stems bearing panicles of pink, deep pink or white flowers. Physostegia, or obedience plant, is a generous bloomer, but many gardeners avoid it because it tends to take over its section of the garden. However, if you can keep it in check, it will provide many weeks of mauve flowers which are excellent for the vase.

Rudbeckia laciniata has tall stems which produce clear yellow, rounded flower heads in late summer. It usually needs to be staked, but does not require special soil, only good drainage and a place in the sun. Salvias come into their own in late summer and there is a large range available with many colours. *Salvia farinacea* is tall and slender with blue or white flowers, while *S. patens* has clear blue flowers. *S. elegans* (pineapple sage) has scarlet flowers and its leaves are edible.

S. sclarea, the well-known Clary sage, a low-growing plant with many slender stems, has variants charmingly called 'Pink Sunday' and 'Blue Monday'.

Shasta daisies, with their open-faced white flowers on straight stems, are a must for every mixed border and will also grow where winters are mild. *Sedum spectabile* is a succulent with grey-green leaves borne on thick stems up to 50 cm tall, and heads of massed, small, pink flowers in summer and autumn. Meadow rue *(Thalictrum delavayi)*, with its

LEFT Osteospermum 'Whirligig', with the centres of its petals strangely folded, is a quaint version of our indigenous osteospermums, and has the typical navy blue centre. Plant it into good garden soil in the sun, give it water when days are dry, and it will happily yield an ongoing harvest of unusual flowers.

fern-like leaves and delicate flowers, will thrive in any shady part of the garden, where it will need rich soil and plenty of water during early spring and summer.

Among our indigenous perennials are gazanias opening to brilliant colours in sunny areas, Barberton daisies (Gerbera jamesonii), Felicia amelloides and pelargoniums.

A blazing beauty for autumn blooming in the warm garden are the anthuriums, some of which have highly decorative large leaves, but are best known for their 'flowers' – the satiny spathes which carry their colour. Anthurium andraeanum has large spectacular spathes, while A. scherzianum has a twisted spadix and smaller spathes. They must have humidity, warmth, water throughout the year (every day in summer; three times a week in winter), and dappled shade in a greenhouse or under large trees out of the wind.

SPECIAL PURPOSE PERENNIALS

FOR SHADE AND SEMI-SHADE
Acanthus mollis (bear's breeches)
Agapanthus spp. (agapanthus)
Campanula spp. (bell flower)
Clivia miniata (bush lily/flame of the forest)
Bergenia cordifolia (heartleaf bergenia)
Begonia spp.
Ferns
Helleborus argutifolius (hellebore)
Hosta spp. (plantain lily)
Ligularia przewalskii (ligularia)

FOR DRY CONDITIONS
Arctotis hybrids (African daisy)
Crassula spp.
Gazania spp.
Gerbera jamesonii (Barberton daisy)
Lampranthus spp.
  (mesembryanthemum/vygie)
Kniphofia praecox (red-hot poker)
Watsonia spp.

TALLER PERENNIALS
Anemone hupehensis (Japanese anemone)
Alstroemeria aurea (Inca lily)
Canna indica hybrids (canna)
Dahlia hybrids
Kniphofia praecox (red-hot poker)
Lobelia cardinalis (cardinal flower)
Phlox paniculata (tree phlox)
Physostegia virginiana (obedience plant)
Rudbeckia hirta (gloriosa daisy)
Verbascum hybrids (mullein)
Watsonia spp.

Ground covers

These living carpets are growing in popularity owing to the demand for low-maintenance gardens. They literally cover the ground, but they do more than that. They bring stability to the soil, they retain moisture and serve as a permanently attractive feature. They also help enormously to keep weeds down.

Many ground covers will cascade beautifully from a container when planted close to the edge. They will also make attractive trailing plants in hanging baskets and window boxes.

Most ground covers are perennials and will be there for a long time, so prepare their site well. As weeds will be difficult to eradicate later, it will be well worth while to follow this method.

First dig over the soil and enrich it with compost and superphosphate to encourage the weeds to come up. Once they have done so, destroy them. Now add some bonemeal to the soil and plant your ground covers.

FEEDING AND MAINTENANCE

Liquid fertilizers should be applied regularly once the ground covers are established to maintain the plants in good condition. Give them a good sprinkling of bonemeal in spring, as well as a top dressing of general fertilizer. Regularly remove dead flowers and cut back untidy growth.

TOP RIGHT *Lamium maculatum, with its leaves of gold and silver, has formed a healthy mat of foliage in the shade. It is a vigorous grower, needing good rich soil which is constantly damp. It can grow beyond its allotted space and should be regularly cut back. The blue-green leaves of* Festuca glauca *are a fascinating contrast.*

RIGHT *Ivy* (Hedera helix) *has been persuaded to cover the ground and the wall, encircling the seat with a tapestry of green, creating a quiet and tranquil retreat.*

FAR RIGHT *Here colours come together with an exciting clash as a curtain of variegated bougainvillea and a carpet of* Tradescantia pallida *'Purpurea' which has spread its purple stems and leaves out in the hot sun. Regular clipping back of the stems will result in healthy growth.*

A WIDE CHOICE

Many kinds of plants make good ground covers and there are suitable plants for every part of the garden, from that hot, sunny bank where arctotis and gazanias will flourish, to the deep shade where ajuga and lamium look good.

Some of them can also be used in the mixed border. For example, a patch of bright yellow sedum spreading out between delphiniums will be startling, and in the shade silver lamium leaves will contrast with bright impatiens.

Seeds of annuals scattered liberally over enriched soil will create colourful ground covers. Among these are alyssum, *Malcolmia maritima* (Virginia stocks) and lobelia.

Apart from annuals and perennials, creeping plants can also be used. Imagine *Trachelospermum jasminoides* (star jasmine) with its glossy dark green leaves and sweet-scented white flowers planted under silver birches or other trees. Ivy too, will happily spread its green carpet under a tree.

ABOVE Lysimachia nummularia 'Aurea', golden creeping Jenny, is a useful ground cover, bringing patches of sunshine wherever it is planted. It prefers full sun, but will grow where it receives the sun for at least part of the day. There is also a green form, while the 'Sunburst' variety is valued for its golden flowers.

GROUND COVERS

SHADE LOVERS

Ajuga reptans (carpet bugle)
Bergenia cordifolia (heartleaf bergenia)
Bromeliads: *Aechmea*
   Billbergia (urn plant)
   Cryptanthus (earth star)
   Nidularium
Campanula poscharskyana (bell flower)
Duchesnea indica (wild strawberry)
Erigeron mucronatus (fleabane)
Helxine soleirolii (peace-in-the-home/baby's tears)
Hosta hybrids (plantain lily)
Lamium maculatum (lamium)
Liriope muscari (lily-turf)
Mazus reptans
Mentha requienii (Corsican mint)
Ophiopogon japonicus (mondo grass)
Pilea spp. (clearweeds)
Plectranthus ambiguus (spur flower)
P. barbatus

Primula x polyantha (polyanthus primrose)
Selaginella kraussiana (spreading club moss)
Trachelospermum jasminoides (star jasmine)
Viola odorata (English violet)

SUN SEEKERS

Arctotis hybrids (African daisy)
Armeria maritima (thrift)
Campanula pyramidalis (chimney bell flower)
Cerastium tomentosum (snow-in-summer)
Cotoneaster horizontalis
Dorotheanthus (Bokbaai vygie)
Echeveria spp. (echeveria)
Erigeron karvinskianus (fleabane)
Festuca glauca (grey-green grass)
Flower Carpet rose

Gazania spp.
Helianthemum nummularium (sun-rose)
Juniperus horizontalis (conifer)
Lobularia maritima (alyssum)
Lonicera pileata (honeysuckle)
Lysimachia (creeping Jenny)
Nepeta cataria (catmint)
Origanum vulgare 'Gold Tip' (oregano)
Oxalis spp.
Phlox subulata (moss pink)
Stachys byzantina (lamb's ear)
Sunsation roses
Syngonium podophyllum (goose foot plant)
Thymus vulgaris (thyme)
Tradescantia fluminensis (wandering Jew)
Verbena peruviana
Viola hederacea (Australian violet)
Viola x wittrockiana (pansy)
Wedelia trilobata
Zoysia tenuifolia (Korean grass)

Annuals

An annual germinates from its seed, grows, produces leaves, flowers and finally, seeds. Then, having achieved its highest purpose, the guarantee of the survival of its species, it dies down. This very transience adds to our appreciation of its seasonal beauty, and every year we plan to welcome annuals into our garden. There are low-growing annuals, and there are even climbers among them. Using annuals freely means you can have a blaze of brilliant colour or a gentle blending of delicate shades.

Quick and versatile

Annuals have so many uses. They can be used to fill gaps in the border; they make a splendid massed display; they create a colourful edging to beds, paths and patios and around garden features; they are invaluable in containers and baskets (see page 95).

There are annuals for the shade and for the sun, and many of them make splendid cut flowers. They bring colour and interest to those spaces between shrubs which are still growing to maturity and they create a pretty ground cover between roses.

In the mixed border annuals can be brought in to coincide with the blooming periods of the perennials, the two blending or contrasting as your colour scheme requires. Annuals are so quick and so versatile. Perennials and shrubs are usually there for a much longer period, but annuals can ring the changes beautifully.

Subtle or striking colours

In summer, combining blue ageratum, torenias and blue *Salvia farinacea* with pale yellow marigolds will be cool and restful; or you can design a veritable festival of warm, sun-drenched colour by planting red salvias, orange marigolds, scarlet celosias and zinnias in close proximity.

In spring, try a serene blending of blue nemesias, nemophila, blue nigella and white alyssum with daffodils and Dutch irises; or go for a more ambitious scheme by bringing in brilliantly coloured mixed nemesias, antirrhinums and petunias or large splashes of pansies and violas. Then brighten your winter garden with annual lupins in a sunny position.

PLANTING TIPS

- Scented annuals include sweet peas, nicotiana, stocks, Virginia stocks *(Malcolmia maritima)*, alyssum *(Lobularia maritima)*, wallflowers and mignonette.
- Climbing annuals create quick colour in the vertical plane. Choose from sweet peas *(Lathyrus odoratus)*, *Cobaea scandens*, *Mina lobata* and *Thunbergia alata* (black-eyed Susan).
- Shady spots are suitable for annuals like impatiens, *Begonia semperflorens*, mimulus, foxglove, coleus and myosotis.
- To dry annuals for use in flower arrangements, choose helichrysum, *Gomphrena acroclinium*, xeranthemum, celosia, lunaria and molucella.
- Popular, rewarding annuals include ageratum, alyssum, amaranthus, anchusa, aster, begonias, celosia, chrysanthemum, cleome, coleus, cosmos, dahlia, delphiniums, dianthus, eschscholzia, gaillardia, gloriosa daisies, impatiens, marigolds, nicotiana, pansies, penstemons, petunias, phlox, poppies, salvias, torenias, verbenas, vinca and zinnias.
- Plant self-seeding annuals such as primulas, alyssum and lobelias.
- Annuals on the very point of flowering are available in bags, which is wonderful for instant colour.

ABOVE *Chinese asters (Callistephus chinensis), are summer bloomers and are highly valued for their flowers which last long in the vase. They may be single or double, and seed or seedlings can be planted in spring, when there is no danger of frost. They will need full sun, rich, friable, well-drained soil and plenty of water.*

OPPOSITE PAGE Papaver somniferum, *the lovely peony-flowered poppy, comes upon the late spring scene dressed in shades of pink, mauve and red, sometimes with petals like shredded paper. When the 'windows' near the top of the seed capsules are open, the seed can be collected, dried, and stored in bottles or packets.*

ABOVE *Violas look lovely on their own, they make good edging plants, and mix readily with other plants in containers, including bulbs. Depicted here are violas of the 'Bambini' series, which has small flowers of diverse colours. Give them full sun, well-dug, well-drained, enriched soil, and water regularly all through the season.*

RIGHT *Solenostemon scutellarioides, better known as coleus, has splendidly coloured leaves of red, purple, yellow, green, pink and shades in between. It is at its best in summer, growing in shade or semi-shade, with plenty of water to keep the leaves healthy.*

Many series, new hybrids

What to plant? There is a wealth of annuals and the range grows continually. It is well worth your while to welcome some of the lovely new colours and forms into your garden. Be brave, try something new, don't stick to the same old thing year after year.

Just think of petunias. There are many series of petunias (look at the name on the tag on each punnet or seed packet) which offer different flower sizes, the presence of veins or white centres or edges, plant heights, tendency to bush or cascade. Then within each series there are many colours. Tolerance to wet weather also differs. This is of great importance in the summer rainfall area, where petunias have a tendency to fall apart in wet weather. These are just some of the most successful series of petunias: 'Cascades', compact 'Milleflora', 'Veined', 'Carpet', 'Madness' with its rich colours, 'Bonanzas' which are exquisite doubles and 'Surfinias', with their wonderful cascading growth of a metre or more.

Then there are violas and pansies, with a multitude of colours and flower sizes, some of single colours, others with fascinating mixtures of colour

on their endearing little faces. The unlikely pairing of deep purple and brilliant orange in the pansy 'Jolly Joker' is just one such daring combination. On a more subdued note, there is the lovely 'Shades of pink' variety.

Sowing your own seeds

Growing annuals from seed not only saves a great deal of money, but it is a fascinating challenge. Hold that infinitely small, brown seed in your hand, then plant it and watch it grow and bloom. See pages 165 – 166 for details on sowing seed *in situ*, as well as in seed trays.

Seedlings

Seedlings bought from garden centres come in compartmentalized punnets and are very easy to handle. As they have been pricked out into a treated growing medium, they generally have developed well. Make sure they are healthy, with green leaves (no sign of yellow), and no spindly growth.

To loosen a seedling from its compartment, either give the container a gentle squeeze, or push a stick (or ballpoint pen) up through the hole at the bottom, and the seedling and its soil ball will be dislodged. This soil ball may have a thick covering of roots, or a thick layer of roots at its base. These

LEFT *Full of impact and certainly not to be ignored is this group of brilliantly coloured amaranthus leaves, single marigolds, and beyond them, making an effort to tone down the startling colours, Salvia farinacea. Summer bloomers and preferring full sun, they all have a long flowering season.*

should be teased out before planting. Plant your seedlings out into damp soil which has been enriched with compost and a slow-release fertilizer, then water them well after slightly firming them in. Some gardeners like to place a handful of chicken manure into the hole and mix this with the soil before planting. This applies particularly to acid soils.

The best time for planting is on a cool, overcast day. If this is not possible, then plant seedlings out in the late afternoon. In hot weather they will need to be shaded with individual caps, leafy branches or with shade-cloth until they are growing well. Of course snails will relish the tender growth. If you put out snail bait, take great care to keep it well out of the way of birds and children by putting it in open-ended plastic tubes or in bottles laid on their sides.

Feeding and maintenance

Once their foliage is flourishing, give the seedlings a dressing of general fertilizer such as 2:3:2 or weak liquid manure (Seagro or Marinure). Water until the soil is thoroughly damp, then allow it to dry out before the next watering. This will encourage the roots to spread out in search of water.

When those first buds appear, enjoy your sense of fulfilment, but remember that it really is better to nip out central buds from poppies, petunias and phlox

(among others) as this will make for a compact plant. At this stage, some gardeners give an application of potassium, to encourage a good crop of flowers. A well-maintained mulch will keep the small plants damp and well fed.

Constant dead-heading is essential to keep annuals in bloom. If the flowers are removed, the plant will produce more flowers, in its effort to create more seed.

Many summer-flowering annuals cannot take heavy frost, so it is better to keep these back in a sheltered place until all danger of frost is over.

FAR LEFT *Golden calendulas and richly purple larkspurs (Consolida ambigua) have been brought together in the early spring garden to put on a brave show of colour, with their leaf textures and heights creating an interesting contrast. Plant them both in autumn, in full sun, and look out for a small green worm which likes to lurk in the heart of the calendulas.*

SPRING-FLOWERING ANNUALS

Anchusa spp. (forget-me-not)
Aquilegia caerulea (flowering columbine)
Bellis perennis (English daisy)
Calendula officinalis (English marigold)
Consolida ambigua (larkspur)
Delphinium grandiflorum (butterfly delphinium)
D. x elatum (tall-growing delphinium)
Dimorphotheca aurantiaca (Namaqualand daisy)
Dianthus barbatus (Sweet William)
Digitalis purpurea (foxglove)
Eschscholzia californica (California poppy)

Lathyrus odoratus (sweet pea)
Linaria maroccana (toad flax)
Lobelia erinus (lobelia)
Myosotis sylvatica (forget-me-not)
Nemesia strumosa (Cape jewels)
Viola x wittrockiana (pansy)
Penstemon spectabilis (penstemon)
Papaver nudicaule (Iceland poppy)
Petunia hybrids
Phlox drummondii (Drummond phlox)
Ursinia anethoides (jewel of the veld)
Venidium fastuosum
Viola cornuta (viola)

Roses

This queen of flowers is prized the world over for its amazing range of colour, beauty of form and often glorious fragrance. There is no doubt that to be brought to perfection, roses need constant attention. But how very worthwhile it is to encourage each bush to do its utter best by giving it sufficient food and water and a permanent mulch, then pruning it at the right time and in the right way.

The rose family

Roses are divided into several groups. First come the two major bush roses: Hybrid Teas (or Large-flowered Bush Roses, with long, pointed buds generally carried singly and not in large clusters) and Floribundas (or Cluster-flowered Bush Roses, which carry informal clusters of roses and fit well into the mixed border).

Miniature roses are also bush-shaped, but are not more than 38 cm in height, with flowers and leaves all to scale. They are wonderful in containers and as edging plants.

Climbing roses encompass Climbers (which develop a semi-permanent structure of shoots) and Ramblers (which do not have this longlasting structure, but send out long, graceful shoots in one season). There are even some Miniature Climbers.

English Roses result from hybridizing modern roses with Old Roses and have the charm of the latter, but now bloom for longer. They are generally available under the name of David Austin Roses.

Ground-cover roses, such as Sunsation and Flower Carpet, are low-growing and can spread more than a metre, forming a lush carpet of colour.

Pruning

Pruning is generally carried out in July, but in areas of heavy frost it must be delayed until all danger of frost is over. See pages 159 – 161 for more details on pruning roses.

Feeding and watering

After pruning comes the only time of the year when it doesn't matter if you disturb the soil around the rose bushes. Gently loosen the soil, water well, then apply a generous mulch of kraal manure or compost or both, but never right up against the main stem. Water the roses again and give them a good sprinkling of fertilizer. To induce a good supply of foliage, which is essential for a fine flush of blooms, apply a fertilizer high in nitrogen, such as 5:1:5 or 8:1:5. Superphosphate and bonemeal can also be added.

In very cold parts gardeners prefer not to put down a heavy mulch during winter as this could keep the ground cold and damp. Once the soil warms up, a mulch is applied. Now settle back and watch your rose bushes grow, giving them a regular drenching once a week until early spring.

ABOVE *Esther Geldenhuys has one of the finest rose gardens in the country, she is an authority on the subject, and has written a book on rose growing. It is fitting, then, that a truly beautiful, sweet-scented, floriferous rose should have been given her name. It is a hybrid tea, with long pointed buds opening slowly to a perfect pink rose.*

OPPOSITE PAGE *'Simplicity' is a generous rose, covering itself with clear pink, small flowers, which open from well shaped buds. Trained against trellis, this 'Simplicity' has been encouraged to show its flowers to their best advantage.*

LEFT *'Claude Monet' is one of the Impressionist roses, each of which has a combination of colours. It's semi-double, with combined splashes of cream and pink, showing a wealth of stamens as it opens.*

More or longer?

In September, much to your joy, plump flower buds will appear. At this stage, you can decide whether you want a good flush of flowers, or whether you would prefer a longer succession of blooms. If the latter, remove a third of the number of rose buds. This sounds rather cruel but those stems will soon decide to produce more buds.

Dead blooms must always be removed with a clean cut just behind the flower.

The first blooms should be picked with short stems so that as many leaves as possible remain. For show blooms, all side buds must be taken off, to allow the large terminal bud to develop into a gorgeous single flower.

Pests and diseases

With the coming of rain in the summer-rainfall areas, fungi such as black spot and mildew will make their appearance. Some of the beetles and aphids may also pay a visit. Even if they have not yet arrived it is wise to start a preventive spraying programme.

Each grower usually has his or her own cocktail of ingredients, but basically each one will contain a fungicide, a foliar fertilizer such as Kelpak, Seagro or Chemicult, an insecticide (if it is really considered necessary), and a wetting agent, all in the appropriate proportions. (*See* page 75 for a few of these spray cocktail recipes.)

Many gardeners are turning away from the chemical insecticides which, as well as dealing with beetles,

BELOW *Sheets and sheets of 'Iceberg' adorn the lawn and stone walls of the house, with shasta daisies and arums bringing their own shades of white.*

THE CYCLE OF CARE

Through the cycle of the seasons there is a programme to be followed to produce healthy foliage and beautiful blooms. With the great diversity of climates in South Africa, it is difficult to lay down strict rules, but these are general guidelines.

- Pruning during the winter (*see* pages 159 – 161) followed by a good feed and water.
- Regular watering and maintaining the mulch cover.
- When the first blooms appear in spring, the roses receive another feed.
- Regular spraying is necessary to keep fungus, and possibly insects, at bay.
- Summer pruning.
- Gradual diminishing of food and water.
- Gorgeous autumn roses.
- Pruning.

LEFT The 'Iceberg' rose has been a winner since it first came upon the rose scene. Here a climbing 'Iceberg' has been planted on either side of the arch into square holes filled with compost and fertilizer.

BELOW A large rock, grey and relentless, has been beautified by a climbing red rose with verbenas as a living carpet. Nearly all the stems arise from the base of the rose.

aphids and others, unfortunately also put paid to mantids, ladybirds and other friendly insects. Try picking off the beetles, or placing insecticide in buckets or tins painted yellow. Beetles always head straight for yellow roses, and so yellow paint will be equally attractive. When aphids attack, dissolve tobacco in water until it is the colour of weak tea and spray the affected plant.

Summer and autumn routine

In the Western Cape, with its Mediterranean climate, roses will need to be watered during the dry summer months.

Summer pruning means getting rid of unnecessary growth and then feeding and watering well. It is also advisable to spray roses at this time to protect them against fungi.

Once autumn's highly coloured roses have come to delight you, keep up the food and water to maintain the plants in good health before pruning. Apply potassium nitrate at the end of autumn, to harden up the wood.

Of course, there are variations galore. Each dedicated gardener has a particular recipe for success with roses, coupled with deep affection for these exquisite flowers.

RIGHT *A pink 'Sunsation' rose has been standardised, and, together with highly coloured lupins, makes a striking picture at the entrance to the drive. Standards should be well staked to keep them upright, and any growth from the main stem below the flowering head should be completely removed.*

ROSE CARE TIPS

- Remove the central bud from a head of floribunda roses to achieve even blooming.
- Young leaves take up a foliar spray more rapidly than do older leaves.
- Some growers recommend the following good 'plate of food' for roses: one heaped tablespoon of 2:3:2, one heaped tablespoon of superphosphates, one heaped tablespoon of bonemeal, one heaped tablespoon of Epsom salts, one teaspoon of L.A.N. Apply this mixture to each bush, then mulch with old kraal manure and water well.
- Never spray on a windy day and take the greatest care of any poisons, keeping them far out of reach of children.
- Some happy companion plants for roses are the low-growing alyssum, *Begonia semperflorens*, violas, petunias, dianthus and pansies. (Many annuals are available in individual colours.) To share the back of the border, select foxgloves, penstemons, delphiniums and verbascum. For edging there are stachys (lamb's ear), cerastium tomentosum, ajuga, lamium and oxalis. Perennials such as lavender, irises, liliums and cineraria maritima go well with roses.
- Always water rose bushes well before spraying, and never spray dried-out bushes.
- Do not plant roses where roses have grown before. If you can't avoid this, an excellent solution is to dig a hole large enough to take a cardboard carton. Place this carton in the hole, fill it with good, enriched planting soil and then plant your rose. It will be established long before the cardboard disintegrates.
- Study each and every rose bush, not with a cold, calculating eye but with deep affection and admiration.

Get to know roses

Roses are so versatile. They can be planted in beds on their own. They will live happily with a carpet of flowers at their feet. There are groundcover roses, roses which will willingly climb up and over arches, or along fences. There are roses which will bloom splendidly in containers. Some have large, elegant blooms, some have clusters of small flowers, some produce tiny miniature flowers. Then there are the graceful standard roses.

Take time to choose your roses. Then give them a good start by planting them in holes at least half a metre deep and wide, filled with soil enriched with compost, superphosphates and bonemeal. A cup of lime should be added to acid soil. They love the sun, but are not keen on strong winds.

Join a rose society or a garden club and discuss the wellbeing of your beloved roses with other rose fanatics. Visit a rose show and you will gather much useful information. Roses may bring occasional heartaches, but they are the source of endless pleasure and a glowing sense of achievement.

To walk in a rose garden with the owner is to hear of the deep affection held for these flowers which are ever-demanding, yet have a worldwide following.

SPRAY COCKTAIL RECIPES

Dilute these chemicals in one or two litres of water, then add enough water to make 10 litres of spraying solution:

- For powdery mildew, light infection of black spot, aphids, bollworm, stem borer, thrips and beetles: 15 ml Funginex, 10 ml Ripcord, 2,5 ml liquid soap or G49, 10 ml vinegar.
- For powdery mildew, aphids, bollworm, stem borer and thrips: 20 ml Citrex or Oleum, 10 g sodium bicarbonate, 10 ml Metasystox, 5 ml liquid soap, 10 g garlic powder.
- For black spot, downy mildew, aphids, bollworm, beetles, thrips and stem borer: 20 g Dithane WG, 2,5 ml Nufilm N, 10 ml Ripcord.
- For black spot, powdery mildew, downy mildew, aphids, bollworm and stem borer: 25 g Bayleton A, 2,5 ml Nufilm, 10 ml Metasystox.
- Other effective fungicides: for black spot – Sporgon (10 g) and Coppercount (20 ml). For downy mildew – Previcure (7,5 ml) and Ridomil (20 g).

ABOVE *'Gold Bunny' standards and 'Rise 'n Shine' miniatures, both of pure gold, are to be seen in Duncan's Roses nursery in Elgin in the Western Cape, where roses are set out in a splendid display in beds and borders and arches.*

LEFT *'Friendship' is a generous bloomer on its neat bush with healthy foliage. In the distance are pink 'Simplicity' backed by white 'Iceberg'. Note the thick layer of mulch laid down between the roses.*

Indigenous plants

Have you ever seen anyone standing with a hose, watering the glorious carpets of daisies in the Karoo? Or an automatic irrigation system spraying a group of clivias nestling on the forest floor? Of course not, for these are part of our wonderful wealth of wild flowers, which are self-reliant, able to develop to wonderful maturity every year, happily adapted to their surroundings.

Why indigenous?

The advantage of indigenous plants is that they will need no more attention than they receive in their natural habitat, but allowance must be made for different climatic conditions in different parts of the country. There are nurseries devoted to the cultivation of indigenous plants, whose owners are only too glad to offer advice on buying and tending our wealth of flora. We often go wrong by expecting winter rainfall flowers to grow where summers are wet and winters dry, and vice versa. But with a little knowledge and encouragement, everyone can have a garden filled with indigenous plants from many parts of the country, with diverse climates, or have them mixed with our exotics. Knowing where they come from helps enormously, and it is well to bear in mind that some plants do not do well away from their natural home, and some do not last as long.

There is an ever-growing interest in indigenous plants for two reasons:

- our growing awareness of South Africa's unique flora and the need to conserve it;
- the desire for low-maintenance gardens, as both leisure time and water become scarce.

ABOVE *Greyia sutherlandii, the Natal bottlebrush, puts forth its scarlet heads of flowers against the clear winter sky when the branches are bare of leaves. A favourite among birds, this shrub can be kept in shape by pruning after flowering. To propagate, half-bury long sections (up to 50 cm) in sand and keep damp.*

OPPOSITE PAGE *Eucomis autumnalis, the unusual pineapple lily, stands sentinel over a mass planting of* Schizostylis coccinea, *white and red river lilies which have stayed close to the water. They die down to make way for winter and spring flowers, then come back in full strength in summer.*

LEFT *White watsonias bloom in spring. There are watsonias for almost every season of the year, with a large colour range and some very good hybrids.*

ABOVE *Aloe barberiae, previously known as Aloe bainesii, is the largest of the aloes, growing into a substantial branching tree as tall as 10 metres. Pink flowers appear in winter, attracting a myriad of birds.*

RIGHT *Gazanias are of the sunshine itself, with their bright, warm colours. There are splendid hybrids which like a place in the sun, with extremely well-drained soil. Propagate them by digging down gently around the plant, and pulling away the side stems, then planting them into clean sand.*

Learn about our plants

There are plants for the hot sun, those for dappled shade, some for deep shade, and topping them all are the mighty trees which grow in the forests and bushveld. With sufficient knowledge and perseverance, we can enrich our gardens with South Africa's wealth of indigenous plants.

Some purists create gardens devoted solely to flora of the region where they live; others combine plants from many parts of the country with diverse climates; yet others successfully mix indigenous plants with exotics.

Knowing something about the natural habitat of various species helps enormously. It's also best to remember that some plants do not do well away from their natural home, some do not last as long and some don't like being moved at all. It is difficult to get a kokerboom to grow once moved away from its hot, desert habitat.

Succulents

Think of the succulents, like the low-growing vygies or mesembryanthemums *(Lampranthus spp.)*, smelly stapelias (carrion flowers) and many others with amazing water-storing stems and leaves. They love the sun and will grow in harsh conditions, although they will do better with a little extra care. Then come the aloes, some growing low on the grassland, others standing tall and proud, sending up their flaming candelabra. Birds love them and just one *Aloe africana* will attract a multitude. Bees cannot resist them either. Many kinds of succulents bloom in winter, some display a lovely colour change in their leaves to brighten the cold days.

Annuals and perennials

Our brilliantly coloured indigenous daisies and daisy-like flowers covering the ground from late winter are world-famous, like the radiant Namaqualand daisies *(Dimorphotheca spp.)*, ursinias, arctotis, Bokbaai-vygies *(Dorotheanthus bellidiformis)* with their vibrant colours, and the endearing annual and perennial felicias. They all grow from seed, which can be generously scattered in autumn and kept damp. They are good mixers and will grow well in pots, or cascade happily over low walls. Our nemesias, together with many of our wild flowers, have been hybridized into a vast range of gorgeous colours.

FAR LEFT *Agapanthus is a most obliging plant. It comes in various heights, in white and shades of blue, and will grow in shade, semi-shade and even full sun, as well as in containers.*

LEFT *'Green Goddess' arum, with its large green-tipped white flowers, thrives in damp conditions.*

BELOW *Pincushions are the easiest of the protea family to cultivate. They need good drainage and will grow well on a slope. Leucospermum 'High Gold' is one of the splendid hybrids developed in recent years.*

Bulbs

The range of bulb and bulb-like plants is bountiful and colourful. Arums bloom in glistening white, pink or yellow and even tipped with green. Agapanthus come in varying heights and different shades of blue, as well as white. Red-hot pokers (kniphofias) hold up their spikes of glowing orange.

Dieramas (harebells) wave on infinitely slender stems, dietes multiply in neat clumps. Gladioli, nerines, clivias, eucomis, watsonias, freesias, ixias and sparaxis all present their gifts of colour and form in spring. They will grow in containers if you are uncertain where in the garden to put them.

Shrubs

There is a wealth of indigenous flowering shrubs which thrive in many parts. Probably the best known are those of our winter rainfall area's fynbos, such as the proteas, leucadendrons and leucospermums. While they do obligingly grow when moved away from their home, it has been found that they do not last as long, and they do need watering in winter.

The pincushions (leucospermums) are easy to grow and will give you a wealth of long-lasting flowers. They must have well-drained soil which should not be disturbed as their feeding roots are near the surface. Give them a good mulch (but no chemical fertilizer) and grow them on a slope. Proteas are a magnet for sunbirds, an exquisite combination.

Some of our indigenous shrubs have attractive leaves, most have lovely flowers, and many are fragrantly sweet-scented, for example September bells *(Rothmannia globosa)*, forest bride's bush *(Pavetta lanceolata)*, wild jasmine *(Jasminum angulare)* and

RIGHT *Strelitzia reginae, the crane flower, bears a mass of handsome flowers from late summer, the flower stems being higher than the banana-like leaves. It should be grown in full sun. Other members of the* Strelitzia *family are* S. nicolai, *the wild banana, and* S. juncea *whose flowers nestle among long, narrow reed-like leaves.*

BELOW *Creamy white* Leonotis leonurus *(wild dagga) and misty mauve* Tetradenia riparia *(iboza) - with a touch of grey* Helichrysum petiolare *at their feet are a soft and gentle adjunct to the early winter garden.*

sagewood *(Buddleja salviifolia)*. Karoo gold or yellow pomegranate *(Rhigozum obovatum)* with their vivid yellow flowers hail from the Karoo and are ideal for dry gardens. Our lovely indigenous ericas offer a range of shades and size of blooms. *Mackaya bella* (forest bell bush or river bells) which produces white trumpet flowers in spring, has the great advantage of growing happily in the shade.

There are many species of plectranthus, varying in size from large to lower-growing, even ground-hugging shrubs, which bear flowers of pink, mauve or white. Most of them come into bloom in early summer, growing in the semi-shade of large trees.

Ochna serrulata, the Micky Mouse tree, is spectacular twice over, as its golden yellow mass of flowers is followed by quaint fruits – with shiny black skin and scarlet calyx – distinctly resembling the famous mouse. *Strelitzia reginae*, the crane flower, has won worldwide acclaim for its outstanding blue and orange flowers. *Tecoma capensis*, or Cape honeysuckle, produces yellow or orange tubular flowers, while *Hypoestes aristata*, the ribbon bush, is covered with mauve flowers in autumn and winter.

Then there is the wide variety of aloes to consider, best planted in groups both for impact and uniformity of care. If you want birds in your garden in winter, plant a group of *Leonotis leonurus* (wild

dagga). It will grow tall and bloom, but can then be cut down hard to make space for other indigenous plants. A grouping of leonotis, aloes, bush violets *(Barleria obtusa)* and *Pycnostachys urticifolia* (blue boys or hedgehog sage) will make a splendid autumn and winter display.

TIPS FOR INDIGENOUS PLANTING

- If you do plan to introduce some indigenous specimens into your existing garden, you may be under the impression that all South African plants are able to withstand dry conditions. This is far from true.
- On the other hand you may find when transplanting small plants from other areas, that they actually do quite well in your garden's more cosseted situation, rather than having to battle for survival amid the scarce resources of their original home.
- It is illegal to remove indigenous plants from the veld.
- If you are establishing a completely indigenous garden, keep everything as natural as possible.
- Make paths of bark chips or pebbles; benches, fences and pergolas of rustic wood; and rock features of naturally occurring, weathered rocks.

Trees

When you think of our very beautiful trees the first to spring to mind are the gigantic stinkwoods and the baobabs with their ridiculous outline.

More easy to handle and more suited to the smaller garden are those with both a good shape and flowers such as the pompon tree (*Dais cotinifolia*) and the Cape chestnut (*Calodendrum capense*) which bring pink-mauve mists of colour to the indigenous forests in summer.

For sweet scent, try a small honeysuckle tree (*Turraea obtusifolia*) with its slender, greenish flowers borne on bare branches in summer. For stark winter splendour, plant a coral tree (*Erythrina lysistemon*); for a froth of springtime blossom, there is *Dombeya rotundifolia* (wild pear). If you're in search of an interesting shape, consider the Natal cabbage tree (*Cussonia spicata*) with its interesting leaves and flowers or the well-loved boerboon or tree fuchsia (*Schotia brachypetala*).

Not to be forgotten are the magnificent yellowwood trees and the thorn trees, the acacias, which are truly of Africa. Visitors wonder at the almost luminous, pale yellow-green bark of the *Acacia xan-thophloea* (fever tree). Plant a thorn tree in your garden and thrill to the sight of it silhouetted against the setting sun – a truly African experience. Some of our indigenous plants will also do their best to protect you from dogs or intruders. A hedge of *Carissa macrocarpa* (num-num or amatungula), lemon thorn (*Cassinopsis ilicifolia*) or *Dovyalis caffra* (Kei apple) have enough thorns to deter any unwelcome visitor.

LEFT Leucadendron argenteum, *our famous silver tree, is well named for its long hairy leaves of silver. It grows well in its native Western Cape, but is usually not happy in other parts of the country.*

BELOW LEFT Dais cotinifolia *bears pink pompons which give it its common name, the pompon tree. It is a small tree, bearing a mass of fragrant flowers in full sun. If grown in the shade, its flowers are sparse and the growth more slender.*

INFORMATION ON YOUR REGION

Local botanists have identified eight large natural communities of flora and fauna in our country: the fynbos, the succulent Karoo, the strandveld, the forest (sub-tropical forest and the Afro-temperate forest of the Garden Route), the bushveld, the thicket, the Karoo and the grasslands. There are suitable trees, shrubs, climbers, herbaceous plants, annuals, bulbs, succulents, reeds, aquatic plants and even lawn grasses for each of these regions.

Many of our wonderful indigenous plants can be seen in our national botanical gardens at Kirstenbosch, Betty's Bay, Worcester, Bloemfontein, Pretoria, Roodepoort, Pietermaritzburg and Nelspruit. Apart from these, there are wildflower reserves in many parts, which are well worth visiting. Find out about them from your local civic office or garden club. You may also like to join the Botanical Society of South Africa, Private Bag X10, Claremont 7735. It offers free admission to gardens, a quarterly magazine, group activities and special seed offers for certain categories of membership.

Contact the National Botanical Institute at Kirstenbosch, Private Bag X7, Claremont 7735, tel. (021) 799 8800, for names of publications which can help you devise a garden best adapted to your region. Ernst van Jaarsveld's *Wonderful waterwise gardening – A regional guide to indigenous gardening in South Africa* (Tafelberg 2000) provides much useful information and planting suggestions for each area of South Africa. Other good references are *Creative gardening with indigenous plants* by Pitta Joffe (Briza) and David and Sally Johnson's *Indigenous trees and shrubs for the South African garden* (Struik).

Food from the garden

Taking a basket out into the vegetable garden to snip off a Brussels sprout and a sprig of thyme, and reaching out to pick a red apple from your own tree, is to know the joy of producing food from your own garden.

Vegetables

Before you take on the exciting task of making a vegetable garden, read books, ask for advice, read the information on seed packets and get the feel of what is involved. Start on a small scale and expand with each wonderful success.

BASIC NECESSITIES

There are several basic necessities when you are planning a vegetable garden, namely adequate water, a sunny, level position, good soil and shelter from strong winds.

Adequate water

The size of garden will depend on the amount of water available. Cabbages, lettuces and other leafy vegetables need a lot of water to keep them succulent. Mulching will reduce the amount of water loss considerably (see page 158).

A sunny, level position

Very nearly all vegetables must have sun for most of the day. A level site allows for easy maintenance of the garden and prevents run-off of precious water. It is worth making the effort to level the ground by setting aside the top soil, levelling the site and then replacing the topsoil.

Set out beds in a north-south direction, about 1,5 m wide, with paths in between them for ease of cultivation from both sides. If there is doubt about drainage, it might be well to make raised beds, holding the soil in with bricks or wood, but providing small drainage gaps at intervals along the bottom of the retaining material.

A long slope can be terraced, or, if this is not possible, separate small areas can be levelled by digging into the slope.

Good soil

Rich, friable, well-drained soil, well-prepared and maintained, is probably the most important factor in the success of the vegetable garden. Once planted, vegetables should not be allowed to look back, so the soil should be well dug and enriched with organics. Preparatory deep digging is strongly recommended. Working in marked-off trenches, set aside

RIGHT *Marigolds are not only attractive interplanted with vegetables, they also help to ward off eelworm and other pests.*

the topsoil, dig over the subsoil to about 60 cm and loosen the soil below that. Replace the topsoil, incorporating organic fertilizer into the top 30 cm. Kraal manure is not as readily obtainable as it once was, and if it is to be used, it should be well rotted.

Compost is invaluable – it improves the texture of the soil, provides food for the plants and, as a mulch, keeps the soil cool and moist.

Soil conditioners are available to improve the soil, and you can buy moisture retainers to help keep moisture in the soil where the plants need it. Chemical fertilizers contain nitrogen (N), phosphorus (P), and potassium (K), obtainable in various ratios, for example 2:3:2 (see page 27).

The main types of vegetables are:
* those whose foliage and stems are valued, such as cabbages, lettuce and celery
* the root crops, including carrots, beetroot, potatoes and turnips
* those producing 'fruit' and seeds, like tomatoes, peppers, brinjals, peas and beans.

Each kind requires its own fertilizer. Nitrogen is essential for the leafy crops, however an overdose of nitrogen will mean weak, watery growth which will wilt badly in hot weather. Phosphorus encourages

BELOW *Here a small garden is filled with good soil and lushly planted with vegetables. As they are growing close together they will need to be harvested early, and the lavender regularly clipped.*

vigorous growth and superphosphate can be used where there is a deficiency (quite often the case at the coast). Potassium is good for the production of healthy plants and fruit. It may also be necessary to supplement trace elements such as molybdenum, iron, magnesium and boron. If you suspect a deficiency, consult your local garden centre or have your soil tested.

Shelter from strong winds

Although vegetables need good air circulation, strong winds can be very destructive. So plant a fence or trellis with beans, cucumbers or granadillas in the path of the prevailing wind, but not too close to the other vegetables to cast shade over them.

WHAT TO PLANT

This depends on your family's preferences. It is no use planting masses of carrots if they are to be spurned. If space is limited, do not plant potatoes or pumpkins or squash. Warm-weather crops include beans, cucumbers, carrots, brinjals, lettuce, melons, peppers, parsley, pumpkins, squash, sweetcorn, sweet potatoes and tomatoes. Cool-weather crops include artichokes, asparagus, broad beans, broccoli, beetroot, Brussels sprouts, cabbages, cauliflower, carrots, garlic, beans (if there is no frost), leeks, lettuce, onions, spinach, Swiss chard and turnips.

HOW TO PLANT

Some seeds can be sown *in situ*, that is, where they are to grow. Take care not to plant too close together, and most importantly, not to plant too many at once. Little and often is the rule. Plant tall crops at the southern end of the bed so that they do not shade the shorter ones.

Among those vegetables planted *in situ* are beans, beetroot, carrots, cucumbers, melons, lettuce, parsley, pumpkin, peas, radishes, turnips, squash, sweetcorn and mealies.

Other seeds are better planted in seed trays or separate compartments and thinned out when the first small leaves appear. Careful sowing of the seeds will mean there is little thinning out to do. The seedlings which are left can be watered very gently and carefully with weak liquid manure (the colour of weak tea). Fend off snails with snail bait or go hunting for them. When the plants are established, they can be given a dressing of fertilizer, and a good layer of mulch which from now on should never be allowed to diminish. Although it is regarded as ideal to rotate crops seasonally to stop the transmission of disease and generations of pests, in a small vegetable garden this is not necessary.

Many gardeners have taken to planting vegetables among their flowers, and it is not unusual to see a gorgeous purple cabbage nestling among the pansies, or an elegant Swiss chard surrounded by nasturtiums. Some of the Chinese vegetables are an attraction on their own.

When combining flowers, vegetables and herbs, bear in mind that if you spray the bed with insecticide the edible crop may be affected.

VEGETABLES IN CONTAINERS

You may long for home-grown produce, but live in an apartment or have a very small townhouse garden. Here containers can be the answer. Pots and troughs are suitable for compact plants and herbs can even be grown in hanging baskets. Climbing plants can be grown on space-saving trellises on a balcony or patio. Some climbing beans are actually very decorative. Quick-growing vegetables such as radishes, spring onions and cress are very rewarding.

The containers must have good drainage. Keep a few prepared pots ready, so that you can sow new seeds (or plant seedlings from the garden centre) while the others are starting to decline.

Prepare the soil well (see page 93) and water at least once a day in summer as containers dry out more rapidly than open beds. As you will be washing out the nutrients, fertilize regularly. Liquid fertilizer is very convenient.

LEFT *A wagon wheel of brick and concrete paving has been laid down in a level area, then filled with vegetables. This makes for easy access, and with just a few vegetables planted in each section, overproduction is avoided.*

Herbs

There are medicinal, aromatic and culinary herbs. All of them have a special charm and, more often than not, a delicious scent or aroma. Getting to know the value of herbs is wonderfully worthwhile. You'll never want to be without them once you have experienced the pleasure of picking and eating a nasturtium leaf or a borage flower, of rubbing lavender between your fingers and inhaling the unforgettable scent.

BASIC NECESSITIES

Most herbs need sun for most of the day, as well as a very well-drained soil. Care should also be taken that taller herbs do not overshadow the lower-growing ones and for this reason it is better to grow them in groups according to kind, with thyme, sage and basil each in its own space. A herb garden can be a joy, be it small or extensive.

HERBS IN MIXED BORDERS

In a small herb garden, there will be little space for the bushier herbs like the lavenders, rosemary and borage, but these will fit readily into mixed borders. While there, consider the popular herbs that are now also available in attractive alternative colour-ings, such as purple basil or golden-variegated sage and thyme. These will be a welcome addition to the colour scheme of your mixed border. Neat, small, non-invasive herbs like thyme, sage and chives also make excellent edging plants, releasing their fragrance when brushed against or side-swept by the mower. Similarly the tougher species of thyme as well as Corsican mint and chamomile, planted between slabs in a path, are a marvellous source of aroma when stepped upon.

HERBS IN CONTAINERS

Herbs grow readily in containers, which means that a large tub or several individual containers can be placed near the kitchen for convenience. What could be nicer than a group of terracotta pots each planted with a herb? Or one of those quaint terracotta strawberry pots sprouting rosemary and thyme, parsley, basil and chives? A small trough on a sunny kitchen window-sill, filled with parsley, chives and sprouting cress, will be pretty and useful.

HERBS AS GROUND COVERS

Many herbs can be used as ground covers. They should mostly not be trodden on, so include some stepping stones and pick your way through a fra-

RIGHT *Lavender and rosemary have been placed in small terracotta pots for an unusual, sweet-smelling table decoration.*

grant little herb walk of chamomile (*Chamaemelum nobile*), Corsican mint (*Mentha requienii*), pennyroyal (*Mentha pulegium*) and wild thyme (*Thymus serpyllum*). Bear in mind that thyme attracts bees, so avoid them if you have young children or anyone with allergies in your household.

Fruit

When planning to bring a new tree or shrub into the garden, we more often then not turn to catalogues of the decoratives, forgetting entirely those which obligingly produce fruit, and often most attractive blossoms.

TREES

An orange or lemon tree next to your patio will add the glowing colour of its fruit to the winter scene for many months, besides giving you blossoms with that typically heady fragrance. One apple tree will yield enough fruit to be eaten fresh, stewed and bottled. A plum, peach or apricot tree will do the same. These are all deciduous and need a cold winter.

Planting and general care and maintenance are much the same as for other garden trees, but *see* page 161 for details on pruning. Before you buy your plant, ask your garden centre about its particular cultivation requirements and eventual height and spread. Each specimen must be given a good start and a continued programme of feeding and spraying for pests. When planting, keep the plant to the same level in the soil as it was in the bag, always ensuring that the graft, if there is one, is above soil level.

TIPS FOR VEGETABLE CARE

- When sowing cress seeds place gauze over the soil's surface to keep the seedlings, which will find their way through it, clean.
- To collect tomato seed for sowing, allow the seed and flesh to ferment for four or five days, then place the matter in a sieve and run water through it until only the seeds are left. Place these on a dry cloth, and, before planting, dust with fungicide.
- Fertilizer granules must not come into contact with the leaves or seeds of vegetables.

BERRY PLANTS

There is also a range of berry plants – such as youngberries, raspberries and loganberries – for growing along fences or between criss-crossed strings or wires. They need good formative pruning and training to establish them. Strawberries, growing by means of runners, ripen to juicy splendour in beds or pots. In the warmer garden you can grow guavas, paw-paws, mangoes, prickly pineapples and, on the larger scale, avocados.

Ideal to train over trellis-work or pergolas are the climbing fruit such as granadillas and grapes (see page 162 for details on pruning).

BELOW *Many fruit trees will fit well into the garden, including orange trees which have a good shape, and bear their golden fruit – both decorative and delicious – for long periods. In the garden setting, they need light, well-drained soil and a sunny position. Calamondins are always either flowering or bearing fruit.*

Specifics & solutions

Special advice is sometimes necessary for a specific task or interest, a certain set of circumstances, or even to help solve a problem. If you have container plants or a shady spot in the garden, a small garden, a pond or a swimming-pool, you may be interested in that particular topic. Advice is also included for enthusiasts with special interests such as a scented garden or a rock garden. The solutions in this section offer help to those gardeners who have to contend with less than ideal conditions, from hot and dry to damp. There are hints and tips galore.

The large rocks in the rock garden have been interplanted with annuals, perennials and small shrubs which, in time, will partly cover them. Wide steps lead from the house to the wide paved area, and the conifer lends height to the sun-drenched scene which contrasts with the shade of the tree on the far side. The thatched roof and rocks contribute to the typical South African scene.

Containers

Just a few pots can make a garden. Containers are so versatile, often so portable, so easy to replant, cosset and then place exactly where you need them. Use them to enhance the garden and patio or to introduce colour in small spaces. Or make them a focal point to link diffferent parts of your garden.

Instant, easy effect

Put an interesting collection of prettily planted containers on the patio, and they will be the first things you and visitors are aware of as you leave the house, marking the transition to the outdoors. Pots can decorate a flight of steps, brighten up a dull corner, create a welcome by the front door, make something special of the pool area.

One daisy bush in a tall pot makes a statement. A shapely and elegant urn with graceful strands of ivy trailing down its pedestal brings grace and dignity to a large garden. Special trees and shrubs are shown to their best advantage in containers. Hanging containers and baskets, suspended from a pergola, roof eaves or against a wall, are an instant method of achieving interest in the vertical plane.

Gardeners with little time, little space, and, more importantly, little water to spare, will find that container planting is the answer. If root interference under large trees makes it difficult to plant, then a few containers will deal with the situation. Admittedly pots need more frequent watering than plants in the ground, but the water is applied right where it is needed and is not unnecessarily dispersed over a wide area.

Containers in many styles

At one time, pot-plants were just that: plants growing in clay pots and even in jam tins arranged in straight rows on the verandah. Now plants in containers are increasingly in demand for every part of the house and the garden, and manufacturers are responding by producing an endless and wonderful selection of pots and dishes and baskets and window boxes in a variety of materials, to help create different styles and atmospheres.

Take a highly glazed pot decorated with Eastern motifs and plant it with a bamboo for an oriental look. Fill a hanging basket with trailing nasturtiums for quaint, cottage-garden appeal. For the modern home, a fitting welcome at the entrance would be a row of mop-top shrubs in tall pots.

It is best to suit your container to the style of your house, contemporary to contemporary, classical to a period house.

Creative choice of plants

Plants, too, come in an endless selection of sizes and growth forms, each fulfilling a particular role in its pot, whether alone or in a combined planting. Some are cascading, some upright, some provide ground cover in the container. There is no need to limit your thinking to everyday houseplants. If a little imagination is used, a beautiful display can be made.

Insert a wire support into the pot or stand it against a trellis and climbing plants can be persuaded to grow as a backdrop for smaller plants. Ferns can be used in abundance for a lush and luxuriant look, and there are many beautiful foliage plants — from large-leafed dieffenbachias, alocasias and maranta to shiny holly *(Ilex spp.)* and fine-textured lippia *(Phyla nodiflora).*

There are few plants which will not grow in a pot, from the smallest of annuals to quite large trees. A good start will ensure that the plants are happy for a long time, with little attention. Look around the garden to see what you can bring into the house and on to the patio. Ground covers will readily take to a shallow container and cascade over the edge. Dig up a clump of violets and ask them to share a tub with a palm tree. An azalea in full bloom can be lifted and placed in a container (incorporating plenty of leafmould), then taken back to the garden when flowering has ceased. Marguerite daisies (*Argyranthemum x hybrids*) look lovely in large pots, so if you have some rooted cuttings (very easy to strike in clean, damp sand, with compost added as they grow), plant them in pots. Nip off a piece of trailing ivy and place it in a hanging basket after pinching out its end growth. Keep back a few of those annuals you are planting in the garden beds, and plant them in a pot in full sun. Make a collection of interesting succulents in a shallow container for a hot spot on the patio.

Citrus trees are lovely on the terrace, producing a heavy perfume as well as golden fruit. *Citrus mitis* (calamondins) bear a crop of small, edible oranges and look attractive underplanted with annuals.

SOIL, POT PREPARATION AND PLANTING

Ensure there are enough drainage holes in the base of the pot, then cover these with curved pieces of broken crockery or largish stones, then a layer of large pebbles, one of smaller pebbles, a layer of leaves and then the prepared soil mix.

Commercially produced potting mix is ideal for containers, but you can make your own. The mix should be porous to allow the water to flow through, but the addition of organic material is necessary to enable the soil to retain moisture without becoming water-logged. Ordinary garden soil is likely to be too heavy, but good loamy soil is ideal, to which can be added good, clean, coarse sand and compost or kraal manure. Seven parts leafmould, two parts sand and one part well-rotted kraal manure is a good mix. Add two tablespoons of superphosphate to every five litres of this mix.

A tree or shrub will do well in the above potting mix, but if seedlings are to be planted around its base, the top layer of soil, about 5 cm, should be a seedling mix. Never plant anything higher than 2 cm below the lip of the pot, for easy watering. For those plants – such as ferns, bego-nias and African violets – which prefer a more porous medium, more leafmould should be added. Vermiculite will lighten a heavy soil. Acid-loving plants will need plenty of compost and milled pine bark.

A mulch will help prevent evaporation and should be added after the first good soaking. After a year or two, gently take off the top layer of soil and replace this with a layer of compost.

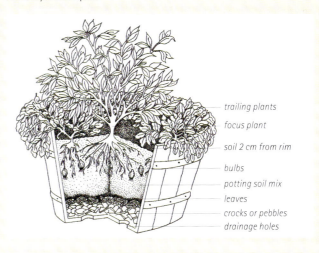

trailing plants
focus plant
soil 2 cm from rim
bulbs
potting soil mix
leaves
crocks or pebbles
drainage holes

ABOVE LEFT There is such a demand for con-tainers that potters and ceramic artists are going out of their way to produce something different, something special, such as this pot with a lizard round its rim.

LEFT Containers need not be planted for them to earn their place in the garden. Well-crafted pots are a decoration on their own, and, well placed, can be a focal point. These pots com-bine beautifully with the pebbles and stones.

RIGHT *'Temple Fire' bougainvillea is more suited to container planting than some others, but too much good food and water will soon see it bursting from its pot. Regularly cut back the stems. The plant, with its top growth reduced, can be removed from time to time and have its roots clipped back before being replanted in its container.*

Fertilizing

There are many pot-plant foods obtainable, including those for special plants such as hydrangeas. Slow-release fertilizers such as Permacote and Sprinkle Grow will ensure months of food supply. Apart from these, superphosphate and bonemeal can be added to the mix – a good handful to a medium-sized pot.

Maintenance

Plants in the garden can survive for fairly long periods unattended, but those in containers need regular attention. They cannot send their roots out into the surrounding soil in search of food and water and are completely reliant on you for sustenance. This should surely give you a feeling of warm satisfaction as you lavish loving care on those very special plants in containers large and small.

Water should be given whenever the top few centimetres of soil are quite dry. A thorough soaking is necessary, not a sprinkling.

When repotting a plant, do not overpot, but plant it into a pot only about 2,5 cm wider than the previous one. The new pot should be only one or at the most two sizes larger.

To save water, a container can be placed in a larger container, the space between filled with damp peat or compost and the planted surface covered with gravel.

Another way of saving water is to place pots on a bed of gravel which is kept moist at all times.

Drip irrigation will save a great deal of water. It may sound tedious to set up a system whereby each pot or basket has its own drip supply, but it is amazing how little water is used with this method. Make sure you have adequate drainage trays under window-boxes and patio containers.

A wire hanging basket

Choose a reasonably sizeable basket made from plastic-coated wire. Line this with coir, moss or a special basket liner. Put in the first layer of a good potting soil enriched with much organic material and mixed with a water-retaining product. Cut X slashes in the lining at regular intervals around the pot at this level and insert trailing plants from the outside through the lining and into the soil. Then add another layer of the prepared soil mix, plant again through further cuts, and top with another layer of soil. Proceed until the basket is nearly full. Then position the last plants on the top of the soil and firm it down, leaving enough space for watering.

Place a fisherman's swivel between the hanging wires and the hook from which the basket is suspended to prevent too much twisting of the wires.

TRIMMING THE ROOTS

Plants may become rootbound. If so, take a long, sharp knife and cut down into the soil about 4 cm in from the edge of the pot. Remove this outer layer of old roots and soil; fill the space with well-rotted compost; water well. The roots will find their way to the new source of food.

Annuals in containers

Containers – and this includes hanging baskets – planted with annuals will bring immediate welcome colour on to the patio, or in the garden itself. They can also be brought indoors for limited periods. Almost any annuals will grow in containers as long as they are given the correct attention.

Good drainage is absolutely essential for the cultivation of annuals in pots, so ensure that the container is properly prepared (see page 93).

Because water, and therefore also nutrients, drain right out of a container, these should be given more often than for plants in the open ground. If the top five centimetres of soil are dry, then it's time for watering. As for feeding, an application of liquid manure or plant food every 10 days will suffice.

Bulbs in containers

All bulbs will do well in containers, as long as they are given excellent drainage and more frequent watering than bulbs in the ground. Prepare the pot by making sure there is good drainage (see page 93), then fill it with friable soil enriched with bonemeal and plant food such as Super 10 or Multifeed. Plant any seedlings first and then the bulbs. Keep the soil damp until growth is well established, then give each container a good soaking regularly.

Hyacinths can be planted in the semi-shade in the garden or raised indoors as splendid houseplants

LEFT *The 'Claude Monet' rose is tall enough to receive the sun, but the impatiens are happy to stay in the shade in this mixed container.*

during their season. To start hyacinth bulbs growing, half-submerge them in a bowl of soil, placing them close together, even touching. Dampen the soil, then store the bowl in a dark cupboard until the first leaves are just appearing.

Alternatively you can place clear or coloured marbles in a glass vase or tube, fill this with water, and then place the bulb so that its base is only just touching the water's surface. Again, store this in a cool, dark cupboard, keep the water topped up and bring it out when there are signs of leaves.

BELOW White impatiens have been wisely planted into the containers to bring light to the shade where the lacy foliage of tree ferns hold back the sun.

TRAILING PLANTS FOR CONTAINERS

Asparagus spp.	*Lysimachia nummularia*
Campanula carpatica	*Pelargonium peltatum*
Chlorophytum comosum	(ivy-leafed pelargonium)
(hen-and-chicken)	*Petunia* hybrids
Cissus discolor	*Philodendron scandens*
Columnea microphylla	*Plectranthus spp.*
Convolvulus mauritanicus	*Rhoicissus rhomboidea*
Epiphyllum spp.	*Saxifraga stolonifera*
Ficus pumila	*Syngonium podophyllum*
Fuchsia hybrids	(goose foot plant)
Gynura sarmentosa	*Tradescantia spp.*
Hedera spp. (ivy)	*Tropaeolum majus* (nasturtium)
Lobelia spp.	*Zebrina pendula*

RIGHT *Lobelias, violas and alyssum (Lobularia maritima) in terracotta pots are in happy companionship against a brick wall, bringing about a charming cottage garden effect.*

OPPOSITE PAGE *What could be better than a splendid display of red roses in white containers to greet visitors to the patio? Although the containers are in full sun, the drip trays ensure that the roses do not dry out, and regular feeding during the growing season ensures a wonderful crop of flowers. The drip trays also prevent water from staining the patio.*

COMBINATION TIPS

- If you are going to combine a tree or shrub with annuals, the pot should be largely filled with potting mix suitable for the shrub, with a layer of seedling mix laid on top for the annuals.
- To create a pleasing composition, mix upright plants with trailing plants. Among the trailers are lobelias, alyssum, petunias, nasturtiums, violas and pansies (also *see* page 95).
- When mixing bulbs with annuals, it is best to plant the annual seedlings first, followed by the bulbs, otherwise the bulbs could be damaged as you dig in to position the seedlings.

- Annuals and perennials go well together, and a hanging basket or a container planted with trailing pelargonium (geranium), *Centauria cineraria* (Dusty miller) and ivy will look lovely.
- Small leaves and flowers are better viewed close by; place bolder flowers, leaves and colours at a distance. Follow the same principle for containers.
- When you have planted your bulbs in containers, sow some Italian rye grass seeds over the top for a pretty effect (it is a controlled environment). The grass can be cut with scissors and later on when flowering is over, it can be pulled out.

Daffodils look most attractive in pots, especially when mixed with other bulbs or annuals.

Excellent combinations can be achieved by layered plantings. Place a good layer of soil in a fairly deep pot, then plant daffodil bulbs. Cover them with soil, then plant another layer of bulbs — more daffodils, freesias or Dutch irises. The leaves will all find their way to the soil's surface and soon you will have a striking display of colour.

Roses in containers

A brightly blooming rose in a pot will create a focal point in the garden, on the patio, even on a balcony. Several pots grouped together will make a real impact. You can place a container of roses into a bed or border to add height or fill a space recently vacated by another shrub or a perennial. When the rose has finished flowering, you can move the container to a less prominent spot.

Roses in pots will welcome companions such as lobelias, petunias, pansies, alyssum, bulbs, erigeron daisies or ground covers. A standard rose with a ground cover rose at its feet is also a lovely sight.

Follow this guide to choosing your size of container. For a single miniature rose: 30 cm wide by 50 cm deep. For two miniatures or one shrub rose: 50 cm wide by 80 cm deep. For a large shrub rose or the combination of a standard rose with miniature or other roses: 80 cm wide by 100 cm deep. In these sizes of pot, the roses should thrive for at least six years. When repotting, use fresh potting soil and prune the roots and foliage.

Prepare the pot well and fill it with the potting mix as described on page 93. Water it well; water the rose in its bag and leave both overnight. The next day, remove half the soil from the pot, place the rose 2,5 cm deeper than it was in the bag (to allow for soil settling) and replace the soil. Add a layer of mulch to the top and leave a gap of about 5 cm between the mulch and the rim. Water well. Water roses in pots daily and fertilize by sprinkling on a tablespoon of 8:1:5 or 5:1:5 once a month and watering it in well. Spray regularly. Remember that roses need at least five to six hours of sun a day.

CARE AND MAINTENANCE TIPS

- Add soil moisturisers such as Terrasorb granules or Hydretain liquid to all containers to improve water retention.
- Terracotta and concrete pots are more porous than plastic, and their plants will need more frequent watering.
- Good drainage is essential. If you feel there are not enough holes in a large pot, place a layer of gravel in the bottom. To ensure good drainage, lift the pot on to special supporting feet, or blocks of stone or wood.
- Crumpled up shade-cloth in the bottom of a pot can act as drainage, as can Bidem, or a special pot liner.
- Charcoal prevents a container-plant's soil from turning sour. Use a large piece of charcoal for drainage or mix smaller pieces with the soil.
- Always add compost to the top of a container. As the layer of compost breaks down, it should be replaced.
- To give a concrete pot a more attractive antique appearance, scratch the surface lightly and paint it over with yoghurt or liquid manure. Put it in the shade and keep it moist, and it will soon grow a mossy coating.
- If your rotary lawn mower has given in, remove the working parts and use the remaining frame, together with its four sturdy wheels, to move heavy containers.

Shade gardening

The cool shade of a spreading tree is a blessing on a hot day and, well planted, will be a favourite spot in the garden. The shade of a wall or the house offers different planting opportunities and with a little thought, the choice of the right plants and proper care and maintenance you can create a shade garden that is a cool, lush retreat, the envy of friends and visitors.

What kind of shade?

Shade in the garden may be cast by trees or walls, structures, or the house itself. It may be dry or damp, it may be morning shade or afternoon shade, or it may be year-round shade on the south side of the house. The kind of shade will affect your choice of plants.

Creating more light

If the shade is under a tree you can try removing some of the offending lower branches, a few at a time. This will create high shade with more light. A fence or hedge causing unacceptable shade can be lowered, if possible.

Near a house or structure, you could paint adjacent walls white to reflect what light there is. Similarly, in a small garden a carefully placed mirror will brighten a shady area, as well as create the illusion of a much deeper garden.

Morning or afternoon shade?

Morning sun and afternoon shade will suit most plants, whereas shade in the morning followed by hot afternoon sun will be stressful for a large number of them.

The reach of shade cast by a wall or a tree will vary according to the season, being shorter in summer, the main flowering season. Plant true shade subjects near a wall and dappled-shade lovers at the fringe of the shade.

Dry or damp soil

One of the problems with planting in the shade of trees is that overhanging branches can actually keep rain from reaching the soil. The tree's root system may also compete greedily for food and water. A garden bed in the shadow of a house may also be in its rainshadow. You will need to compensate by watering well and mulching. Alongside the house you could put a line of fine sprinklers covering the area of the rainshadow. Once you do water regularly, however, you will find that in shady areas not as much water is lost through evaporation.

Damp shade, deliciously cool, is found in a hollow or sunken garden or in a secluded section where shrubs shade lower-growing plants. Many shade-loving plants enjoy the moist conditions in these areas, but if the spot is very damp and the air circulation is restricted, the soil may turn sour. Dig it over several times and add plenty of organic material. For very wet conditions, drainage pipes may have to be sunk into the ground.

The combination of shade and damp promotes the growth of moss and algae on the ground and on paths and steps, which could make them slippery and cause an accident. Scrub them with soap or a solution of copper sulphate (one teaspoon copper sulphate to five litres of water).

In damp, shady parts of the garden also watch out for fungal diseases, which are more frequent where air movement is restricted.

ABOVE Aeonium arboreum *shows off its neat rosettes of leaves. This is one of the few succulents which relish the shade.*

OPPOSITE PAGE *Clay pots partly hidden by fern foliage supply water to the shallow dish, from where it runs over and on to pebbles and peace-in-the-home* (Soleirolia soleirolii), *kept ever damp in the shade of a wall. Bromeliads provide bright splashes of colour.*

Depleted soil

Greedy tree roots tend to take a lot of nutrients from the soil. Don't give up. With a few clever structural adjustments you can provide well for your shade plants. You can do a little root pruning and dig in large amounts of compost and other organic matter to help retain moisture. But this is only a temporary measure.

For smallish plants you can create space between large roots by trimming the smaller offshoots of the roots, removing soil, lining the hollows with black plastic sheeting pierced for drainage, and filling them with a fertile loam before planting.

For bigger plants you can make very attractive built-up beds from dressed stone or facebrick in subdued, variegated shades. Large tubs — for shrubs like hydrangeas — are an equally good solution. Protected in one of these ways, your precious shade plants will get the water and nutrients they need.

Although acid-loving azaleas and camellias may appreciate the occasional shower of pine needles, bear in mind that pine needles could be harmful to other plants.

ABOVE Fuchsia triphylla has an upright growth form and interesting green-bronze foliage. Its red tubular flowers contrast boldly with the paler shade of impatiens and pansies, all of them perfectly happy in damp, shady conditions.

PLANTING BETWEEN TREE ROOTS

Trim the smaller offshoots of large roots, remove the soil between them, line the hollows with black plastic sheeting pierced for drainage, and fill them with a fertile loam. Place small, shade-loving plants in the prepared space and water well.

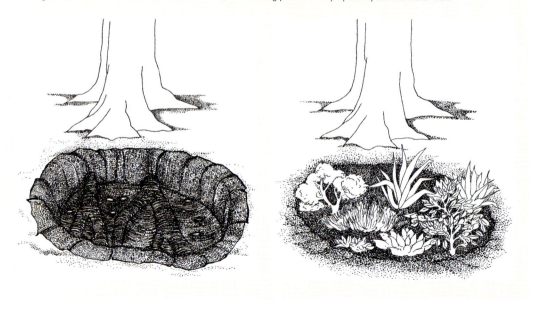

Other factors

Shady spots can be cooler than open, sunny areas. This is an advantage in some climates, but in cooler regions the growth of plants may be slower in the shade than in sunny areas.

A shaded area may also experience other stresses. For example the shady strip next to the house might also be a high-traffic corridor for many passing feet. Here a creative solution might be to plant some shade-loving shrubs or perennials right up against the house, lay down attractive railway sleepers with interplanted groundcovers for the passing traffic, and then train a shade-tolerant climber such as honeysuckle over the boundary fence.

Plan your planting

The key to success is, as always in landscaping, to choose those plants which are suited to the particular environment. Some plants are very happy to grow in the shade, for which nature has adapted them. Others will tolerate semi-shade and even do well, as long as their other requirements are fully provided for. Flowers which bloom in the sun will be pale, but interesting, in the shade.

Shade provides much scope for creativity, for combining heights and shapes, textures and colours.

The glory of green

There are many shades of green and so many attractive foliage plants which are natural shade-lovers. Textures vary widely, so mix them with abandon. Ferns range in size from the delicate maiden-hair fern *(Adiantum raddianum)* to the broad-leafed bird's nest fern *(Asplenium nidus)*. Then move up to the tall tree ferns, of which the Australian species *(Cyathea australis)* grow faster and are more heat tolerant than our indigenous ones *(Cyathea dregei)*.

The aspidistra is a true shade lover and the Victorians called it the cast-iron plant because it could endure adverse conditions. Other shiny-leafed plants which reflect and increase the dancing, dappled light that filters through are alocasias, acanthus, clivias, agapanthus and arum lilies.

Complete your composition of greens by planting selaginella, ajuga or *Soleirolia soleirolii* (peace-in-the-home) and ivy to form a soft carpet underfoot.

ABOVE *Kept in check by low wooden logs are alternanthera, New Guinea hybrid impatiens and Solerolia solerolii (peace-in-the-home) backed by syngoniums and ferns, creating a cool and colourful corner.*

LEFT *A golden Euonymus japonicus and a silver grevillea bring light to the shady corner where the water is fringed with ferns and fuchsias, and the giant leaves of a philodendron are patterned against the shadow.*

Variegated foliage

Variegated plants can light up a shady spot, but many will lose their bright colours through lack of sun. A variegated hibiscus (*Hibiscus rosa-sinensis* 'Cooperi') with white and pale green leaves would perform well, and an aucuba would continue to produce its eye-catching green leaves spotted or splashed with gold. You could also select a golden fern, for example *Nephrolepis bostoniensis* 'Boston Gold', and a golden syngonium for its trailing habit.

For ground cover, the attractive silver- and gold-splashed lamiums such as 'White Nancy' and *Lamium maculatum* 'Golden Anniversary' are really low-growing. *Ajuga reptans* 'Atropurpurea' and 'Variegata' will grow well in light shade and ground polygonum (*Polygonum capitatum*) will spread enthusiastically.

TIPS FOR SHADY AREAS

- When container plants are suffering from too much sun in mid-summer, give them a temporary break in a shade-dappled spot where they can recover and at the same time lighten and liven up the area.
- Place a statue, urn or Japanese stone lantern amid a sea of greenery in a damp, shady spot so that its pale elegance serves as a focal point. Moss will cling to it in time, giving it an authentic, aged appearance that adds mystery and romance to the garden.
- One of the best ways of dealing with an area shaded by a tree with invasive roots is to pave it and fill it with containers planted with shade-loving plants.

Flowers for shade

Brilliant azaleas, serene hydrangeas, dainty fuchsias: those are probably everybody's top-of-the-mind choice. You will find that the lighter colours show up better in the shade. Plant white and soft pink impatiens, the taller varieties in groups and the low-growing ones as edging. The lovely white *Lilium longiflorum* and wind anemones also add height to a bed, while climbers carry their colour even higher. Honeysuckle (*Lonicera x heckrottii*) with its fragrant, pale yellow and pink-purple flowers, is tolerant of shade. The star jasmine (*Trachelospermum jasminoides*) will both climb and spread as a ground cover.

Blue in the shade is most effective – imagine a cloud of myosotis, or pansies, or violas. Add a touch of white and the whole picture sparkles, as you will see when you plant a carpet of pale blue and white Australian violets. For a collection of vivid mauves freshened with white, plant cinerarias in the part-shade. Don't forgo the joy of seeing primulas trace a froth of pretty pastels across a lightly shaded bed in late winter and early spring.

Aquilegias and foxgloves have an old-fashioned charm, while angelicas with their tall stems and green flower heads make a striking statement. Other unusual plants are the hellebores with their deeply lobed leaves and cup-shaped flowers.

Begonias are well-known for their tolerance of shade. Rex begonias are low-growing plants with highly coloured leaves, while the tall tree begonia carries bunches of flowers on slender canes. The annual *Begonia semperflorens* will produce its pink, white and red flowers in partial shade as well as in sun, provided it gets plenty of water.

Although many flowers are more often found in sunny conditions, they will also grow in light shade, where their colours will be paler. Day lilies are just one example.

Caring for shade plants

Plenty of moisture and a humid atmosphere are necessities for most shade-lovers, so water them well and spray the leaves to keep them healthy. Lay down a good layer of mulch and replenish it as it breaks down.

Check that roots of trees are not crowding out the specimens you have underplanted and take remedial action. Replenish nutrients regularly as they will be washed through with much watering, and the plants may also have to compete with the roots of trees and larger shrubs.

PLANTS FOR SHADE, SEMI-SHADE AND LIGHT SHADE

ANNUALS
Aquilegia caerulea (columbine)
Begonia semperflorens (wax/bedding begonia)
Digitalis purpurea (foxglove)
Impatiens walleriana (Busy Lizzie)
Mimulus luteus (monkey flower)
Myosotis alpestris (forget-me-not)
Primula malacoides (fairy primrose)
Torenia fournieri

PERENNIALS AND BULBOUS PLANTS
Acanthus mollis (bear's breeches)
Alocasia macrorrhiza (elephant's ear)
Anemone hupehensis (wind anemone)
Aspidistra elatior (cast-iron plant)
Astilbe x arendsii (goat's beard)
Begonia rex (painted leaf begonia)
Bromeliads
Caladium spp.
Clivia miniata (bush lily/flame of the forest)
Colocasia hybrids (elephant's ear)
Crocosmia aurea (montbretia)
Ferns

Helleborus niger (Christmas rose)
H. orientalis (Lenten rose)
Hosta hybrids (plantain lily)
Primula x polyantha (polyanthus primrose)
Rehmannia angulata
Scadoxus multiflorus katharinae (Catherine wheel of Natal)
Thalictrum delavayi (meadow rue)
Veltheimia bracteata (forest lily)

CLIMBERS
Hedera spp. (ivy)
Jasminum spp.
Lonicera spp.
Monstera deliciosa (delicious monster)
Parthenocissus quinquefolia (Virginia creeper)
Philodendron spp. (philodendron)
Syngonium podophyllum (goosefoot plant)
Trachelospermum jasminoides (star jasmine)

SHRUBS
Aucuba japonica (Japanese laurel)
Camellia hybrids

Daphne odora (winter daphne)
Euonymus japonicus (spindle tree)
Hydrangea spp. (hydrangea)
Mahonia spp.
Philodendron selloum (split-leaf philodendron)
Rhododendron hybrids (azaleas)
Pieris spp. (andromeda)
Strobilanthes dyerianus (Persian shield)

GROUND COVERS
Ajuga reptans (carpet bugle)
Bergenia cordifolia (heartleaf bergenia)
Chlorophytum comosum (hen-and-chicken)
Duchesnea indica (wild strawberry)
Lamium maculatum
Liriope muscari (lily-turf)
Lysimachia nummularia (creeping Jenny)
Ophiopogon japonicus (mondo grass)
Pilea spp. (clearweeds)
Saxifraga stolonifera (mother-of-thousands)
Selaginella kraussiana (spreading club moss)
Soleirolia soleirolii (peace-in-the-home)
Syngonium podophyllum (goosefoot plant)

The small garden

A small garden has its own challenges to meet. Whether you want a profusion of flowers, a low-maintenance garden, a space where children may run free, or an extensive leisure area, careful planning will be necessary to use all available space in the best possible way.

Preparation and planning

Aspect is of greater importance in a small garden than in a large one and each section should be put to good use according to the amount of sun it receives. In a small, walled garden there may be extremes of temperature. The hot sun may bake some areas, but never reach others, so plan and plant accordingly. An open brickwork wall will allow air to circulate, but still give reasonable privacy.

A north-facing patio which will be warmed by the winter sun and, if your garden is really hot in summer, a shady outdoor retreat on the south side of the house will be welcome. An east-facing garden will receive gentle morning sun, whereas a garden facing west will receive hot afternoon sun.

Paving and other elements

Paving can create useful spots, perhaps where smaller plants won't grow in the shade of large shrubs or a small tree. Paving which is laid below the damp course of the house will look good if a uniform material is used for paths, patios and raised beds to create a flowing unity, rather than a disparate, patchwork look. There are many shapes and colours of paving available and it would be well not to go for bright, hot colours and hectic patterns as these can be distressing in a small space. Rather choose the tranquillity of grey.

Paving neatly laid will be a permanent feature and spaces left in the paving can be planted with various ground covers, annuals or other plants.

A path running across a garden will make it look smaller. However, the look of a long, narrow garden will be improved if a path is laid across it.

Containers holding an attractive mix of upright and trailing plants can give height, serve as a focal point or soften the area where patio blends into garden. Outdoor chairs and tables will double your entertainment area and a trellis will bring shelter and seclusion.

DESIGN TIPS

- A small garden should match the house in structural materials and texture. It should be an extension of the house, easily accessible, and much lived in.
- Changes of level will add interest.
- Walls and hedges in the garden itself will be an invitation to go around them to see what is on the other side, making the garden appear larger and adding mystery and the element of surprise.
- Do include some vertical elements here and there, otherwise no sense of depth is created and the eye is drawn straight to the boundary. A small tree or a climber over a pergola would be a good idea.
- Planting greenery to conceal a garden wall ensures that the boundary is undefined and the garden looks larger. Use non-rampant climbers on trellises if shrubs would reduce the size of the borders.
- Use small plants and flowers to keep your design in scale.
- Good foliage and long-blooming flowers are essentials for small gardens, as you want every square metre to look good, year-round.
- To save space, vegetables can be planted among flowers.

ABOVE *A splendid example of exquisite and perfect proportion in a tiny garden. Dark green euonymus balls are set in a sea of echeverias around the bird-bath. Splashes of colour come from begonias and a tall verbascum offset by a clipped box hedge.*

OPPOSITE PAGE *Exotic indeed is this small corner. Bromeliads (Nidularium spp.) with bright, shining crimson centres enfold a blue glazed ceramic pot to create a slightly oriental look. The blue of the pot is echoed by the flowers of 'Royal Cape' plumbago. Then it's back to Africa with the clay bowl and birds. Each plant and piece has been placed with extreme care and thought.*

BELOW *The space between house and street wall is less than two metres, yet hosts a garden of great interest and beauty. Shaded for most of the day, the area has been planted with clivias, white impatiens and dark mondo grass (Ophiopogon planiscapus 'Nigrescens'), with creeping Jenny (Lysimachia nummularia) between the paving stones.*

For children – or not?

If children are to walk and play in your garden, don't grow plants with thorns or prickles, as these are hard to avoid in a small space. For peace and harmony it is often better to make plentiful play space for the young ones your primary consideration. So make generous provision for lawn and paving, and keep your special plants in a small area set apart. If you can fit it in, a wooden wendy-house will bring endless pleasure and can be used later as a garden shed. Enjoy watching your children in the garden – these years are precious indeed and will fly by, never to be retrieved.

If children are not a primary consideration, there is a range of choices.

- It is possible to pave a small garden completely, creating steps to bring changes of height, placing a formal pool in the centre and using pots planted with shrubs as almost sculptural decoration.
- A compromise between a real lawn-and-plants garden and a courtyard garden would be to devote a small garden entirely to a variety of well-chosen shrubs, interlaced with gently curving paths leading one between and beyond.
- You could design (or commission) a severely formal small garden, with strictly geometric shapes, and plants kept in constant check. Bear in mind that lines must be straight, levels true and upkeep meticulous.
- Probably the simplest, most classic design places a grassed or paved area in the centre, with bor-

COLOUR TIPS

- Use colour to create the illusion of a larger garden. Keep the more vibrant colours near the house, progressing to paler shades further away. While shades of blue create a misty, far-distant illusion – a strong colour at the end of the garden would unfortunately emphasize its limit.
- In general, pale colours make an area appear larger.
- Strong colours like orange and red are often disturbing in a small garden.

ders on either side and, at the far end, a small shrubbery or a raised terrace shaded by a small tree. There are many possibilities, each one calling for meticulous planning.

Pointers for planting

This is a deeply personal matter, but in a small garden each and every plant must be made to earn its place, with shrubs chosen for good-looking foliage and flowers year-round. Rampant perennials are not welcome, nor are shrubs which spread themselves beyond their allotted space, or trees whose roots reach far and wide.

Trees will naturally have to be on the smaller side, and their position and size will affect their surround-

ings. A tall slender tree will bring vertical interest and possibly act as a focal point, while a lower spreading tree will create its own micro-climate. Instead of small trees, some gardeners prefer to use tall standard shrubs, enjoying their decorative qualities but using large umbrellas for shade. Choose your small tree with care, avoiding those which cast heavy shade, rather going for lightly leafed trees which let a shimmer of light through. Ask for advice and look at other gardens, for once a tree has grown it will be hard to take out.

The lawn in a very small garden can be troublesome as it determinedly spreads its roots, but it can create a tranquil, cool effect. Rampant grasses should be avoided and those with fine leaves encouraged.

OPPOSITE PAGE TOP A large variety of plants has been grouped in a small space, to interesting effect. They range from tall, slender fever trees to fat, round cycads and conical golden conifers, with perennials filling the space between them. In the foreground mounds of purple pansies frame the entrance to the paving which is interplanted with mondo grass.

LEFT Who said walls were dull? Here a lichen-covered stone wall is framed by ficus standards accompanied by two small mopheads and an attractive low border edged with dark mondo grass.

ABOVE *In a townhouse garden interplanted paving leads off the patio, to a small pool. A cycad adds a note of drama to this sheltered, secluded retreat.*

RIGHT *This mirror in the wall never ceases to amaze visitors. Set in a dark green wall in a shady spot, it reflects back the sunny part of the garden, with bewildering results. The wire geese were placed in front of the mirror to prevent visitors from trying to walk through into what they think is another part of the garden. It's a perfect – and perfectly charming – illusion of space.*

ILLUSION TIPS

- If your completely concealed boundary blends seamlessly with your view of trees in surrounding gardens or on the street, you are in fact 'borrowing' this outside view and creating the illusion of a much larger garden.
- Fix a mirror at least the size of a normal door to the garden wall, perhaps softening its edges with a few sprays of creeper. The mirror will reflect greenery and flowers and create the illusion of an opening through to another section of garden.
- You can buy arched trellis panels which are designed to appear to recede in the centre. Fix one or more to a creeper-clad wall, perhaps placing a mirror or a graceful statue in the centre. The false perspective will make the garden appear larger.
- A skilfully painted trompe d'oeil mural on a garden wall can portray a rural or garden scene with wonderfully deep perspective, all in two dimensions!
- Paths can be built so that they grow narrower as they lead away from the house, again artificially enhancing the effect of perspective.
- A line of pots which decrease in size as they lead away from the viewpoint will similarly enhance the impression of distance and space.

Features

Most gardeners want to bring in some form of decoration to the garden. In a small garden the choice of these is of vital importance. One sizeable statue placed at the end of the garden will look elegant, but a scattering of gnomes and small statues would create a disturbing effect.

A water feature will bring cool, blue reflections and, if the water is moving, the tranquil sound of droplets splashing down. Make your water feature formal or informal to suit your overall plan.

The use of a mirror or mirrors will give an illusion of depth to a small garden and draw the eye away from the distraction of surrounding buildings or other structures. Lights in a small garden will enhance the concept of its being part of the home.

Attractively shaped containers are a boon to small garden owners, serving as a decorative statement as well as a home for all kinds of plants. They can be planted with shrubs, annuals and even herbs and vegetables.

LEFT *Where two walls meet and cast their shade, a series of shallow bowls have been used to make an interesting water feature. A magnificent Asparagus densiflorus 'Myersii' sends up its thick, green cylindrical cat's tails alongside the sleeper-paved path.*

TREES AND SHRUBS FOR SMALL GARDENS

Acalypha spp.
Acer buergerianum (Chinese maple)
A. negundo (box elder)
A. negundo 'Variegatum' (variegated box elder)
A. palmatum (Japanese maple)
Apple tree
Betula pendula (silver birch)
Camellia spp.
Citharexylum quadrangulare (fiddlewood tree)
Citrus spp.
Codiaeum spp. (crotons)
Conifers
Coprosma spp.
Cordyline spp.
Cussonia spp. (cabbage trees)

Dais cotinifolia (pompon tree)
Diospyros whyteana (bladder nut)
Euonymus japonicus
Fuchsia hybrids
Gardenia jasminoides
Ginkgo biloba (maidenhair tree)
Halleria lucida (tree fuchsia)
Hibiscus rosa-sinensis
Hydrangea spp.
Ilex aquifolium (English holly)
Ixora coccinea (flame of the woods)
Koelreuteria paniculata (golden rain tree)
Lagerstroemia indica (pride of India)
Magnolia soulangiana
Malus floribunda (Japanese crab-apple)

Murraya exotica (orange jasmine)
Nandina domestica 'Pygmea' (sacred bamboo)
Olea europaea africana (wild olive)
Phormium tenax (New Zealand flax)
Pittosporum eugenioides (lemonwood)
P. viridiflorum (cheesewood)
Prunus spp.
Rhaphiolepis indica (Indian hawthorn)
Rhododendron spp. (azaleas)
Robinia hispida (rose acacia)
Rothmannia globosa (September bells)
Spiraea japonica 'Anthony Waterer' (pink may)
Tibouchina spp.
Viburnum macrocephalum (Chinese snowball)
V. odoratissimum (sweet viburnum)

Pool planting

The pool may be tucked away, separate from the main garden, or it may be an inherent part of it, its paving continuing out into the rest of the garden where trees and shrubs share their shade with the pool area.

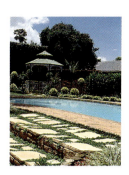

What to achieve

The swimming-pool is an important part of the entertainment area in a garden – make it as attractive as possible. The choice of plants to be placed around the pool is a personal one, but there are useful guidelines to follow. What you need to achieve is a beautiful way of integrating the pool with the garden, plus seclusion, shelter from the wind, shade in the correct spots and privacy.

Paving, drainage, fencing

If the approach to the pool is by means of steps, there should be no soil in between the steps. In fact any link – paths, paving, steps – between house and pool should have a clean surface so that soil will not be walked into the pool. You can edge a path or patio with annuals and flowering perennials, but this is not a good idea around the pool itself. Here evergreen shrubs, foliage perennials and ground covers are best grown. Annuals can be most successful in containers though, giving you bright colour without loose soil to mess up your nice, clean pool.

Any planting should be done in such a way that there is no danger of soil escaping on to the paving or into the pool. Low walls, preferably with drainage at the base, can be the solution.

Drainage is important and garden beds and paving should slope slightly away from the pool, so that hose-water or rain does not wash soil into the pool. With a saltwater pool it is important that the water from the pool does not wash into the beds,

so you may need to put a drain around the pool to prevent this.

Some wise parents place a security fence around the pool. This is not a thing of beauty, and planting to soften its effect is a challenge. The answer could be low containers, placed on the outside of the fence, some of them planted with delicate, evergreen climbers, so that you can still see through the fence for safety reasons. But make sure that the container does not provide a handy step-up for a child trying to climb over the pool fence. On the side away from the house, the fence can be more densely planted, but heavy climbers should be avoided.

While a lovely soft lawn is considered an ideal neighbour for a pool, do ensure that there is at least 1,5 m of paving between the two to prevent lawn clippings being walked or blown into the pool.

Trees

The sun needs to reach the water to warm it, which means tall trees should not be planted on the north side of the pool unless they are sufficiently far back, so that while they do create a screen, their shade does not reach the water.

Shade will be in demand near the pool and although a summer house will give shade, it can be quite hot. If you choose a tree with a spreading umbrella shape it will give cool shade, but it should be far enough away from the pool not to drop its leaves right into the water, nor cast its shadow on the water.

ABOVE *With the spaces between the paving stones planted, there is no danger of soil being taken into the pool. The gazebo brings shade for swimmers, and topiary trees seen against a dark background are an attractive addition to the pool area.*

OPPOSITE PAGE *A cool, shady path of stepping stones nestling amid ground cover leads past leafy shrubs to a dramatic, dark pool. Strelitzia nicolai (wild banana), palms and other sub-tropical shrubs, together with the large man-made rock in the foreground, add to the natural jungle theme.*

It is often said that deciduous trees should not be planted near the pool because they shed all their leaves once a year. But it may be worth considering the fact that while deciduous trees get rid of all their leaves at one time, this is in autumn when swimming is not so frequent. Evergreens shed their leaves all through the year.

Shrubs

Evergreen shrubs are an excellent choice. (See pages 39 – 49 for discussion of shrubs.) Those bearing flowers are not suitable, as flowers attract bees and fallen blossoms can cause slippery conditions. Fruit-bearing shrubs and trees are similarly dangerous.

Plants with thorns should be kept right away as there is always a danger of slipping on the paving and tumbling into the clutch of thorny branches.

Coprosmas are an excellent choice as they are available in upright or spreading shapes and offer attractive shiny green foliage or leaves variegated with green and yellow or white. Their neatness of habit is another plus. Serene lavender bushes, cool grey foliage with mauve, blue, even pinkish blooms are popular with garden landscapers.

TREE TIPS
- Avoid trees with invasive root systems as they could damage the pool, its paving and its water supply.
- Ensure that you keep branches of nearby trees trimmed back so they do not overhang the pool and burden the filtration system with more leaves than necessary.

RIGHT Impatiens and gaura line the sleeper steps from the house down to the pool, which has been well-designed to fit into its surroundings. The lawn is edged with rope tiles to prevent soil from washing on to the brick paving. Bright colour is provided by a tibouchina, ixora and the leaves of acalyphas, while the foliage of tree ferns, cycads, palms and dracaenas brings added interest.

A tropical look

There is no doubt that palm trees and cordylines have a place near the pool, as their growth is slender and they hold fast to their leaves. Palms have comparatively compact root systems and established palms can therefore be transplanted with success to give your pool that instant, tropical garden look. Do check the light conditions required by the palm you have set your heart on. While most enjoy sun or semi-shade, a few prefer the shade.

Ferns will also contribute to a tropical theme and not all of them insist on shade. Consider a tree fern such as *Dicksonia antarctica* (soft tree fern) for example, which is evergreen, has long fronds and eventually develops a sturdy trunk. Its leaves can be removed as they die down. *Strelitzia nicolai* (wild banana) will grow tall and dramatic, its long fronds bringing a lushly tropical look.

Containers & rock gardens

Containers are attractive around the pool and can be planted with small shrubs, perennials, trailing plants and annuals. If they are placed on pedestals they could be knocked down in boisterous play and cause great harm. Give them drip trays, so that soil does not wash out and into the pool.

A rock garden can create a lovely natural backdrop to your pool. Try to choose cool, grey rocks to blend with the blue of the water and ensure that none are jagged, to avoid accidents.

Keep the construction low and make sure that the soil is firmly contained in the pockets created by the rocks. If necessary a rock garden can have a low wall at its base and a drain or gutter to lead away excess water.

Landscaping ideas

Some pool owners like to place plants (those which do not drop their leaves) so close to the water that the plants practically hang over it – on one, or even two, sides of the pool. These planting areas must preferably be away from the link with the entertainment area, on the side where traffic is low and a backdrop will have most impact.

If your house and garden design is formal, creating elegant straight lines of planting alongside the pool will echo your style, and the colour of the water will emphasize the cool restraint. A dark-lined pool can be especially dramatic.

If you have a narrow space between your pool and a boundary wall, try clothing the wall in ivy or star jasmine (*Trachelospermum jasminoides*) or plant shrubs with slender growth such as cordylines or palm trees. If the area is in the shade you can completely fill it with plants such as ferns or alocasias. Or you can try phormiums, coprosmas, agapanthus and spathiphyllums. An elegant solution is a row of pots with slender plants, or shrubs clipped to lollipops or trained as standards.

BELOW *One end of this pool is completely shaded where ferns flourish, and water is fed over well-laid rocks. A peninsula with a round pot marks the transition into the sunny part of the pool and garden.*

The scented garden

When sweet fragrances fill the air in a garden, we feel refreshed, serene, at one with nature. Growing and nurturing scented plants will add another dimension to your garden.

Lifts the spirits

What joy to walk in a garden where scented plants live, to suddenly catch the perfume of a weeping sage *(Buddleja auriculata)* or a holly-leaf osmanthus *(Osmanthus fragrans)*, to brush past a brunfelsia with its fragrant flowers of purple, lilac and white. And is there anything to touch the perfume of a deep red rose such as 'Papa Meilland', 'Oklahoma', or 'Crimson Glory', or a carnation with its spicy clove scent? They all give generously of their perfume, allowing it to waft into the air.

Other plants have leaves which must be crushed to release their aroma. Lavenders, rosemary, lemon verbena and thyme are among these.

Citrus trees such as lime, lemon, grapefruit, mandarin and orange all bear blossoms with a heady perfume. The shiny green leaves of these attractive ornamental trees are also fragrant.

There is no doubt that inhaling the fresh aroma of crushed lemon verbena leaves lifts the spirits and makes one feel good. In fact fragrant plants are always a worthwhile addition to the garden. Their diversity is enormous, from low-growing mint releasing its clean scent in the shade, to the giant magnolia tree with its huge flowers up to 25 cm in diameter.

Roses are legendary for their scent and have always been grown as much for their fragrance as for their beauty.

Ideal situation

Some positions are ideal for scented plants. Place specimens whose scent is released when their leaves are crushed, along paths and steps, or in pots on the patio where they will be brushed by passers-by. In the mixed border, keep flowers with sweet fragrances such as roses and lilies within reach, at the front of the border, together with annuals such as wallflowers, stocks and alyssum.

The patio is a wonderful place to sit in peace amid the scented glory of well-chosen plants – in standing containers, in hanging baskets conveniently at nose height, or as climbers over pergola or trellis. Imagine the pleasure derived from a mixture of mints and violets in containers under a heavily scented pergola covered with jasmine or honeysuckle.

Popular container subjects with fragrant flowers include narcissus, hyacinths, freesias, alyssums, violets

FRAGRANT ROSES	
DAVID AUSTIN ENGLISH ROSES	Memoire
Ambridge Rose	Mister Lincoln
Chaucer	New Zealand
Sharifa	Oklahoma
The Prince	Papa Meilland
Troilus	Sheila's Perfume
	Stephanie de Monaco
	Zulu Royal
HYBRID TEAS	
Bewitched	FLORIBUNDAS
Blue Moon	Bavaria
Casanova	Courvoisier
Double Delight	Friesia
Duftwolke	Manou Meilland
Just Joey	

ABOVE *The tall and slender* Rothmannia globosa *tree, a member of the gardenia family, looks rather ordinary until September, when a myriad creamy bell-like flowers release their heady perfume into the air – hence the common name, September bells. It cannot take heavy frost, and needs a friable and fertile soil.*

OPPOSITE PAGE Brunfelsia pauciflora, *the well-known yesterday today and tomorrow was given its name because its flowers open to purple, then fade to mauve and finally to white. It is one of the most popular scented plants since just one bush will bring fragrance to a large part of the garden. Here it has been used as a hedge.*

RIGHT *Wisteria sinensis* *spreads its fragrance far and wide. Clusters of flowers are borne on the bare branches of this deciduous climber before the leaves appear in summer. Wisteria is renowned for 'taking over' its place in the garden – keep it in check by removing straggling growth and cutting side stems back to about 30 cm in autumn.*

BELOW *Tall white translucent* Lilium longiflorum *flowers tower over the blooms of 'Double Delight' roses turning a shady corner into a fragrant haven.*

OPPOSITE PAGE TOP *'Crimson Glory' has been with us for a long time but still has a great following, for its strong perfume and for its flowers of deep red velvet. There is also a 'Crimson Glory' climber.*

OPPOSITE PAGE BOTTOM *Scented* Stephanotis floribunda *has a neat growth form with twining stems and dark green leaves. In spring it sends out its creamy waxen flowers which have a strong fragrance. It will not take heavy frost, but will grow in a container in a sheltered part of the garden or on a patio.*

SCENTED ANNUALS

- Alyssum *(Lobularia maritima)* has a distinct scent of honey, particularly when warmed in the sunshine.
- Mignonette *(Reseda odorata)* bears summer flowers with an old-fashioned scent.
- The tobacco flower *(Nicotiana alata)* is grown for its lovely evening fragrance.
- Wallflower *(Cheirantus cheiri)* produces star-shaped flowers in winter and spring.
- Stocks *(Matthiola incana)* are worth the extra effort to ensure healthy flowers.
- Sweet peas *(Lathyrus odoratus)* will fill your house with their delightful scent.

and orange jasmine *(Murraya exotica)* and those with fragrant leaves include penny royal, lavender, rosemary and bergamot.

Some plants are particularly fragrant at night. Their perfect position is outside your bedroom window or, again, on the patio. Imagine, after a hard day's work, relaxing in the moonlight under a Chilean jasmine *(Mandevilla laxa)* in full bloom. Surely its heavenly fragrance will waft away life's cares and bring you a little closer to the wonder of nature.

SCENTED PERENNIALS

- Carnations and pinks both have a typical clove scent.
- Chrysanthemums bring a spicy scent to the autumn garden.
- Freesias send out a heavy, heady fragrance particularly in the evening.
- Hyacinths have a heavy perfume when they bloom in spring.
- Scented geraniums *(Pelargonium spp.)* have fragrances reminiscent of apple, rose and nutmeg, among others.
- Plant peppermint, Corsican mint *(Mentha requienii)* or pennyroyal between paving stones as a herb walk.
- Lemon thyme *(Thymus citriodorus)* has an especially sharp, fresh aroma.
- The white Saint Joseph's lily *(Lilium longiflorum)* and the Madonna lily *(L. candidum)* have the strongest fragrance among the liliums.
- The most delightful of the mint family is the eau-de-cologne mint *(Mentha x piperita* 'Citrata').
- Catmint *(Nepeta faassenii)* with its aromatic leaves and mist of mauve flowers makes an excellent bushy border to a path or driveway.
- The tall, waxy flowers of tuberose *(Polianthes tuberosa)* have a typical white flower fragrance.
- Violets or *Viola odorata* have a delightful old-fashioned fragrance.

SCENTED TREES, SHRUBS AND CLIMBERS

Abelia floribunda

Aloysia triphylla (lemon-scented verbena)

Brunfelsia pauciflora 'Floribunda' (yesterday, today and tomorrow)

Citrus varieties

Daphne odora

Gardenia jasminoides (gardenia)

Heliotropium arborescens (heliotrope)

Heteropyxis natalensis (lavender tree)

Jasminum angulare (wild jasmine)

J. multipartitum (starry wild jasmine)

J. nudiflorum (winter jasmine)

J. polyanthum (Chinese jasmine)

Laurus nobilis (bay tree)

Lavandula spp. (lavenders)

Lonicera spp. (honeysuckle)

Magnolia grandiflora

Murraya exotica (orange jasmine)

Osmanthus fragrans

Pavetta lanceolata (forest bride's bush)

Philadelphus coronarius (mock orange).

Plumeria rubra (frangipani)

Rosmarinus officinalis (rosemary)

Rothmannia globosa (September bells)

Trachelospermum jasminoides (star jasmine)

Turraea obtusifolia (small honeysuckle)

Viburnum x burkwoodii

Wisteria spp.

The rock garden

A rock garden is by no means just a heap of rocks thrown together with a little soil between them. To create a worthwhile and attractive feature in the garden, rocks and a variety of plants must be brought together to enhance one another in as natural a way as possible. The word 'natural' is the key to rock garden construction, with stones laid down in just the right way, holding secure pockets of nutritious soil.

Position

With its tiered effect a rock garden presents a good view of all its plants. These need not all be drought tolerant. Pockets of colourful annuals, cascades of trailing plants, compact cushions of ground covers and the occasional tall plant can join together in a harmonious composition.

The ideal spot for a rock garden is on a slope. If this is not possible, then a low construction of not more than a metre and a half can be backed on to a wall. A rock garden can be made on a level area, but it would have to be really low and gently undulating to look at all acceptable within the rest of your garden design.

As its plants are encouraged to trail and flow and fill the pockets with colour, a rock garden will not fit well into a formal garden. To deal with a slope in a formal garden, it would be better to build terraces separated by straight walls. Alternatively, a hedge or wall can separate the main formal garden from the rock garden.

Construction

The best rocks are those which are well-weathered. In some areas you are not allowed to remove rocks from their natural surroundings. However, farmers are sometimes glad to have rocks cleared off their fields, so make enquiries.

For the sake of uniformity rocks should be all of the same structure and colour, but they should vary in size for an interesting, natural effect. Artificial rocks should not be ignored, as they are easy to handle and you can choose your shapes and sizes.

Rocks should be laid down as flat as possible and should not be allowed to stick up into the air like sharks' teeth. They should be seen, but not allowed to be too obtrusive, so bury them to about half of their depth, slightly angled so that the rainwater runs back into the good-sized pockets of soil you place between the rocks.

A single rock with several crevices for soil and plants can be transformed into an attention-grabbing rock garden. Choose small plants with compact growth but different shapes, accompanied by one or two cascading species.

ABOVE *A great variety of interesting plants can be brought together in a rock garden. Here weathered, lichen-covered rocks are kept company by echeverias, kalanchoe and sedum.*

OPPOSITE PAGE *Conifers and cordylines have been used as screening plants. Below them a pool of* Nandina domestica *'Pygmaea' in autumn scarlet separates the grey-green of the* Hebe pinquifolia *from the golden conifer. At the base, rocks show through the planting of annuals. This grouping of plants was wisely chosen to tolerate the extreme winter cold of the Free State.*

Starting at the bottom, lay out your first row of rocks in flowing lines, firming them well into the soil. Fill the spaces behind these rocks with good soil, pressing it in so that there are no air pockets. On to this base you can now place your next row of rocks. Take care not create boring straight lines of rocks, but do ensure that their strata all appear to run in the same direction and that the weathered sides of the rocks face outwards. Do not proceed with the next row until you are quite happy about your progress so far. Keep checking your construction from all angles and also walk right back through your garden to see what your rock creation looks like from a distance. If you include any paths, make these of subtly toning stepping-stones or stone chips.

A rock garden should be an integral part of the garden. You should consider allowing water to flow through yours, to add more interest and pleasure.

Soil preparation

The best possible soil should be used and it must be well drained and between 20 and 30 cm deep. It is a mistake to make the soil pockets too shallow. Heavy soil will be difficult to handle in the smaller pockets, so add plenty of compost and sand to heavy soil. Light, sand soil will need plenty of compost. Adjust the balance of the soil to suit the plants you choose, perhaps adding dolomite for those which need lime, and peat moss for those preferring an acid medium.

Planting

The aim should be to create a series of small gardens enclosed in rocks. There are many, many plants which will be happy to grow in a rock garden, and in fact they relish having their roots in the shelter of the rocks. Some will make cushions, some will cascade, some will grow upright. Cascaders can be planted at the lower end, with one or two of them placed in the centre or at the top of the garden, for interest. Rosette-shaped plants like echeverias look charming in crevices.

Check the eventual height and spread of your plants and avoid those with invasive roots. Plant specimens at any time of the year, except the coldest months in frosty areas. Firm them in well and top-dress them after planting.

Care and maintenance

Having made your rock garden, look after it well by watering when appropriate especially during hot, dry and/or windy weather. Replenish the soil constantly (adding bonemeal and milled compost in spring), dig out weeds before they get too firmly established, clip back those plants which need it, and replace any which are not making a contribution to the overall picture.

PLANTS SUITABLE FOR ROCK GADENS

ANNUALS

Ageratum houstonianum (floss flower)
Anchusa capensis
Anemone coronaria (poppy anemone)
Arctotis fastuosa (African daisy)
Begonia semperflorens
Bellis perennis (English daisy)
Dimorphotheca hybrids
Portulaca grandiflora (moss rose)
Tropaeolum majus (nasturtium)
Ursinia anethoides (jewel of the veld)
Verbena hybrids

PERENNIALS

Achillea filipendulina (yarrow)
Agapanthus spp.

Agave attenuata
Aloe spp.
Anigozanthos flavidus (kangaroo paw)
Aquilegia spp. (columbine)
Artemisia spp.
Babiana stricta (bobbejaantjie)
Chlorophytum comosum (hen-and-chicken)
Drosanthemum speciosum (vygie)
Echeveria hybrids
Erigeron karvinskianus (fleabane)
Eucomis autumnalis (pineapple flower)
Felicia amelloides (kingfisher daisy)
Geranium incanum (carpet geranium)
Gerbera jamesonii (Barberton daisy)

Kalanchoe spp.
Kniphofia spp. (red-hot poker)
Lampranthus spp. (vygie)
Limonium spp. (statice)
Nierembergia hippomanica
Ochna atropurpurea (carnival bush)
Osteospermum ecklonis (river daisy)
Pelargonium spp.
Sedum pachyphyllum (jelly beans)
Sparaxis tricolor (harlequin flower)
Watsonia spp.
Zantedeschia spp. (arum lily)

SHRUBS AND GROUNDCOVERS

Ajuga reptans (carpet bugle)
Barleria obtusa (bush violet)

Cistus hybrids (rock rose)
Convolvulus sabatius (ground morning glory)
Cuphea ignea (cigarette bush)
Erica spp.
Gazania hybrids
Juniperus conferta
J. horizontalis 'Wiltonii'
Lavandula spp. (lavender)
Pimelea rosea
Punica granatum 'Nana' (dwarf flowering pomegranate)
Reinwardtia indica (yellow flax)
Rosmarinus officinalis (rosemary)
Tecoma capensis (Cape honeysuckle)
Tradescantia spp.

Water features

Once they were called ponds or fishponds, then pools. Now they are water features, growing enormously in popularity, their range of size, shape, style and purpose limited only by the garden designer's imagination. An area of still water brings an air of peace and tranquillity, with beautiful reflections of garden and sky. Water can also flow and cascade, spray and tinkle, its sound and sight having a cool, calming effect.

Size

A water feature need not be large or elaborate. Even a shallow bowl of water on the patio will contain its own reflected picture.

A stone bird-bath, on a pedestal or simply placed among the plants in a flower bed, will attract birds and have the same calming effect as a more elaborate construction.

In order to circulate water, both submersible and surface pumps are available. Ask your garden centre about the various methods of creating a whole new world of flowing water, by way of streams, falls, cascades, gentle bubbles and fountains. Note that it may be necessary to obtain the services of an electrician to install the pump, as the correct materials and procedure are important when combining electricity and water.

Ready-made ponds

These are usually made from asbestos cement or fibreglass and are by far the easiest to install.

All you do is create a completely level area and place the ready-made pond on it, standing on bricks, so that you can mark its outline on the ground beneath. Then dig the hole you have outlined, to the depth of the pond plus 5 cm. When all stones, debris and roots have been removed, spread out a 5 cm layer of sand on the bottom and position the pond firmly on this. A piece of old carpet underfelt will also do very well.

Check that the pond is level, with a straight edge and a spirit level, otherwise the water will always run to one end. Make sure the lip is just above soil level, so that rainwater and mud do not flow in.

Backfill the space left with soil, firming it down and checking that the pond remains level as you proceed. Use attractive stones or paving to conceal the lip of the pond and insert a fountain with a pump as a finishing touch.

Many water feature kits are obtainable, usually in the form of two or three irregularly shaped ponds placed so that water flows from one to the other. Their scale varies from something quite small that you could tuck among your patio plants, to larger sets that could blend into a shady, woodland corner of the garden. These kits come complete with pumps and pipes and are simple to install.

SAFETY FIRST!

A child can drown in a few centimetres of water, so consider carefully whether you should have a water feature if you have small children or grand children at home. Young lives are priceless. You may decide to postpone acquiring that feature until they are older. If you do go ahead, please make proper arrangements for the security of your precious children, grandchildren and other little visitors. One safe alternative is to buy an ornamental fountain with several tiers. Water flows over on to pebbles below, and is then pumped up again, so there are no stretches of collected water at all.

ABOVE *Strong jets of water shoot up from almost ground level to create an unusual candy-floss effect of fine silken threads catching the light. Pebbles disperse the water before it is sent once more on its way.*

OPPOSITE PAGE *An ambitious water feature well executed. A natural look results from careful positioning of the rocks, some of which overhang the water, and the fact that the source of water for the cascades has been partly hidden. Palms, cordylines, cycads and ferns bring many shapes and shades of green to the tranquil stretch of water.*

Plastic-sheet lined pond

You can also make a large pond, lined with plastic. This choice is more durable and means that you can dictate the size and shape of your pond. But don't choose too complex a shape, as it will be difficult to fit the lining comfortably.

Mark out your shape with rope and dig the hole, sloping the sides inwards and leaving a few reasonably sized shelves about 25 cm deep for marginal plants. In its centre the pond should be about 45 cm deep. Having dug your hole, make sure there are no sticks or stones as possible hazards, then put down a layer of sand. On top of this you can place under-felt or fibreglass insulation material cut to size, or you may place the lining down straight away. Obviously before you cut the plastic sheeting, measure the pond and allow for a good overlap on to the ground surface around the pond. Fold the cut sheeting in half, placing the fold along the centre line of the pond. Then very carefully spread out the liner, taking out any creases as you go. Place stones along the edges to keep the liner down, perhaps cementing stones together to keep them from moving. Finally fill the pond. Sunlight can damage the liner, so keep the pond filled at all times.

Animals' claws, plant containers and children can easily damage the liner. A useful and natural-looking method of protection is to cover the part of the liner which extends over the rim of the pond with pebbles. Reconstituted stone slabs are also useful for this purpose.

TIP FOR WINTERTIME

Ponds can freeze over in winter, but please don't tap the surface with a hammer to break the ice, as this could shock the poor fish. Rather place tins of boiling water on the surface to make holes in the ice. Freezing over can sometimes be prevented by leaving a plastic ball or a piece of pool noodle in the water during winter.

MAKING YOUR OWN PLASTIC-SHEET LINED POND

Mark out the shape and dig a hole with several shelves shallower than the centre.

Line the hole with plastic sheeting, generously overlapping. Half-fill to settle the liner.

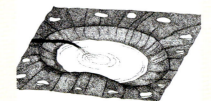

Arrange stones or pebbles around the edge to keep it down. Stones can be cemented.

Reinforced concrete ponds

For a very large pond or series of ponds, you will probably go for a concrete lining. For very large ponds, steel reinforcing may be necessary. A level sand bed is prepared, then a vinyl backing laid down, then the concrete. This is especially useful when you are planning cascades. The walls of the pond could also be built from bricks and covered with a special coating for waterproofing. A drainage outlet leading to a suitable point should be left in the concrete floor. Whenever the pond is drained, it should not be left empty for more than two or three hours since it may crack if it dries out.

Concrete lined ponds, should be filled, left for about a week, then emptied and refilled before fish and plants are placed in them. This is to get rid of any substances which could be detrimental to fish.

Seek professional advice or employ a contractor if you are not confident that you can handle a construction of this nature by yourself.

Planting and populating

Don't be alarmed if the water in your pond initially resembles thick pea-green soup. This is caused by algae, which love their new home's sun and warmth, and all the minerals which are in plentiful supply in the water and in the soil used for the plants. These algae will multiply enormously, but should disappear after a time, as the food diminishes and the plants (within and beside the pond) grow to shade the water. Changing the water could start the whole process again, so it is worthwhile having patience. Oxygenating plants (see page 128) will help to keep the water clear.

When you plant, you should keep more than half the surface of the water clear of plant foliage and flowers, so ensure that your oxygenators do not take over. These plants are, however, good friends to fish. They absorb the carbon dioxide which the fish give off and in turn release oxygen into the water for the fish themselves to breathe.

BELOW *Pebbles lining a pool and spreading out on to the surround create a natural look. This effect is best in shallow water where the pebbles can easily be seen. A shallow pool lined with plastic is a quick way of making a water feature, apart from which the pebbles will protect the plastic lining from damage caused by dogs and children.*

RIGHT Even a small water feature can bring about an atmosphere of peace and calm. Unseen are the workings of this charming feature where terracotta is the predominant colour and the green of the lion and his basin is echoed in the planting of water irises and restios.

BELOW Eastern elegance is the hallmark of this tranquil pond with its typically oriental decoration. The large jar stands perfectly level so that water can flow evenly down its sleek sides.

Fish are not only beautiful, but useful. They eat mosquito larvae, other insects, worms and snail eggs. Koi are currently very fashionable and this is a whole world where the experts will advise you on depth of water, flow of water, feeding and so on. Before you take on these exotic oriental beauties, learn all you can about their requirements. Ask pet shop owners and your garden centre to help you choose which kind of fish will be best for you.

Gold fish are much easier to care for and guppies or mosquito fish, as their name implies, are adept at keeping mosquitoes down. As aeration is essential, make sure that your oxygenating plants are established before the fish arrive.

Fish should never be dumped straight into the water after they have been brought home. Place the container in the pond and leave it until the temperatures inside and outside it have equalized, then allow the fish to swim gently into the water.

In late spring and summer you will surely hear the sounds of courting frogs and toads, their croaks, whistles, squeaks and whoops. They can be a pest, but there is virtually nothing you can do about them, apart from covering the pond with frog-proof netting. If you are agile, you could try to catch them, but if you don't want them to come back, you will have to take them a long way away.

What is the solution? Become a frog watcher. Go out with a torch to see what is happening. You will see fat toads, slender reed frogs, elegant ranas, each battling to get its call into that moment of silence following the call of others, each with that absurd air bag inflating and deflating. Get to know the whistle of a red frog, the mournful whoop of the walking frog, the staccato pips of the striped rana. Or invest in a pair of earplugs.

WARNING
Water lettuce *(Pistia stratiotes)*, water hyacinth *(Eichhornia crassipes)* and pickerel weed *(Pontederia cordata)* are declared invaders and may not be cultivated in the garden.

LEFT *This concrete pond is not very large, but there is enough space for a water lily to show its pretty pink flowers. Mauve ground morning glory (*Convolvulus sabatius)*, punctuated by balls of golden privet, cascades down to the water's edge.*

Plants

These are generally divided into deep-water plants, marginals and oxygenators. Plant them soon after purchase. When preparing them for planting, work in the shade to prevent the plants from drying out and experiencing heat stress.

DEEP-WATER PLANTS

These include the lovely *Nymphaea spp.* (water lilies) and are planted in special plastic baskets or plastic plant pots with holes drilled in sides and base, lined with clean hessian. Special aquatic soil can be purchased, and some slow-release, preferably high-phosphate, fertilizer added.

Firm the plant into the pot and top the soil with a layer of stone chips to weigh it down and keep the soil from floating out. In the deepest part of the pond stack sufficient bricks so that when the basket is placed on them the leaves reach the surface of the water. Then, as the plant grows, you can remove a brick or two.

Do not introduce young plants into the pond in winter in very cold areas. Tropical water lilies will not take severely cold conditions, when they should be taken out, have their leaves cut and be kept in a bucket of shallow water in a sheltered place. Don't be tempted to plant too many water lilies, or they will surely take over the pond.

PLANTING A BASKET

Line basket with hessian and fill with aquatic soil and slow-release fertilizer. Position the plant, add more soil and firm down. Weigh down with pebbles or stone chips and trim hessian.

BELOW *A wooden barrel which has been water-proofed with plastic and provided with its own small fountain lends height and interest to its shady corner. Philodendron 'Xanadu' forms a dramatic back-drop and grassy Acorus gramineus 'Variegatus' grows happily with its feet in the water.*

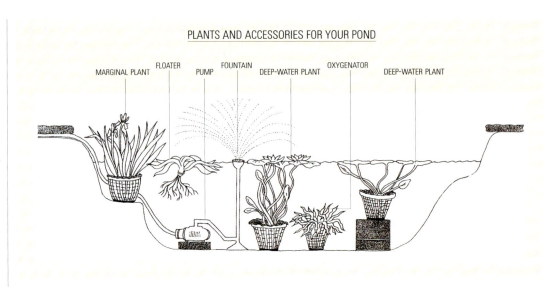

PLANTS AND ACCESSORIES FOR YOUR POND

MARGINAL PLANT — FLOATER — PUMP — FOUNTAIN — DEEP-WATER PLANT — OXYGENATOR — DEEP-WATER PLANT

OPPOSITE PAGE *The Nelumbo lotus will bring its splendid serenity to any warm garden. Settle it at the edge of the water where it will take root in the marginal soil, or plant it in large containers sunk into the water. Where winters are cold, it can be grown in containers which are brought out of the water, and the soil kept just moist until all danger of frost is over.*

MARGINAL PLANTS

Marginals, shallow-water plants which like to have their feet in the water but their leaves and flowers largely above, include water irises, gunneras, papyrus and others. Plant them in baskets like the deep-water plants and place them on the shelves incorporated in your pond construction, or pile up more bricks until there is no more than about 8 cm of water above the roots. Try indigenous bullrushes and ask farmer friends to pass on a few other indigenous plants growing in the shallows of their dams.

OXYGENATORS AND FLOATERS

Oxygenators are plants which stay submerged in the water, releasing their valuable oxygen into the water, not into the air, and thus doing a great job of keeping the water in good health. Although they can be planted in a bit of soil at the bottom of the pond, if there is any, it is best to plant a few pieces in each of several small baskets or pots, weighed down and submerged. This stops them taking over the pond.

Floaters drift on the surface of the pond to reduce algae and provide shade.

WATER PLANTS

FOR THE WATER'S EDGE
Acer spp. (weeping maples)
Acorus gramineus
Ajuga spp.
Astilbe spp.
Bergenia spp.
Carex spp.
Cyathea dregei
  (tree fern)
Dissotis canensis
Ferns
Hosta spp.
Iris spp.
Pennisetum spp.
Phormium tenax
Salix mucronata
Schizostylis coccinea
Selaginella spp.

Tradescantia virginiana
Wachendorfia thyrsiflora
Zantedeschia spp.
  (arum lilies)

DEEP-WATER PLANTS
Nelumbo spp. (lotus)
Nymphaea spp. (water lily)
Nymphoides indica (water
  snowflake)

MARGINAL PLANTS
Acorus gramineus
  'Variegatus' (sweet flag)
Cyperus alternifolius
  (umbrella sedge)
Cyperus papyrus (paper
  reed/papyrus)

Gunnera manicata
Houttuynia cordata
Iris laevigata (water iris)
I. pseudacorus (yellow flag)
Sparganium erectum
Thalia dealbata
Typha latifolia capensis
  (Cape bullrush)

OXYGENATORS
Elodea canadensis
  (Canadian pondweed)
Vallisneria spiralis (eel grass)

FLOATERS
Aponogeton distachyos
  (waterblommetjie)
Lemna minor (duckweed)

Special conditions

Some sections of your garden may be just a bit more challenging than others: a hot, dry bank; a damp, low-lying patch; or unsightly structures which must be concealed. Or you may have a coastal garden with sandy soil and salt-laden prevailing wind. The hints and advice in this section will certainly help to alleviate the problems of these areas and may just show you what unique opportunities they present for the resourceful gardener.

Coastal gardening

How wonderful to have a view of the sea, with its ever-changing colours and movement and moods. But how distressing to have salt-laden spray affecting your plants, and to have wind blowing nearly all the time, leading you to wonder whether it is worthwhile trying to garden at all.

EXPLORE THE NEIGHBOURHOOD

It is worthwhile, it really is! Gardening almost on the beach brings with it all kinds of challenges, but just a few hundred metres away, there is world of difference. Before you give up altogether, explore your area to see what your neighbours are doing, and you may be invited to have tea in a sheltered bower or windowed summerhouse looking out to sea. Alternatively, ramble along a beach walk to see what plants grow under sandy beach conditions. Visit a nearby park and talk to the gardeners there.

IMPROVE SANDY SOIL

Sandy soil allows water to run through untrammeled, so something must be done to stop its flow. Compost and leafmould come to the fore here, which must not just be sprinkled on the surface, but dug deep down into the soil.

Try to create trenches. Go down to half a metre, difficult though this may be, and then lay down a good layer of leafmould or vegetable peelings. Another very good alternative is to lay down a thick layer of newspaper which has been lightly torn, not shredded. Gardeners have even been known to put down pieces of underfelt. Then fill the trench with good soil, mixed with the sand. When it is not possible to do this on a large scale, individual holes can be made, or even large containers of metal or plastic with holes punched in the bottom, can be let down into the ground and filled with good soil.

Always put plenty of mulch around plants. Avoid fertilizer which is high in nitrogen as this could help produce leaves which are too lush and thus vulnerable to wind.

A NATURAL WINDBREAK

To keep the wind at bay, don't think of a wall, which will only push the wind up over the top to create destructive turbulence on the other side. However an artificial windbreak made from slats, latticework or breeze-bricks might work.

ABOVE Haemanthus coccineus, *our indigenous paintbrush, so called for its head of small flowers enclosed in dark bracts, blooms before its leaves appear. It prefers shade or semi-shade and dies down in winter.*

OPPOSITE PAGE *Sleeper steps, planted with heliotrope, wallflowers, euphorbia and irises, a gently sloping path leading to more steps flanked by a strelitzia – these turn a slope into a lovely feature. A nearby orange tree extends welcome shade and an invitation to relax on a wooden bench.*

TREES FOR COASTAL GARDENS

Alberta magna (Natal flame bush)	*Halleria elliptica* (wild fuchsia)
Archontophoenix cunninghamiana	*H. lucida* (tree fuchsia)
Brachylaena discolor (Coast silver oak)	*Harpephyllum caffrum* (wild plum)
Calodendrum capense (Cape chestnut)	*Mimusops spp.* (milkwood)
Citharexylum quadrangulare (fiddlewood)	*Pandanus utilis* (screw pine)
Dais cotinifolia (pompon tree)	*Sideroxylon inerme* (white milkwood)
Delonix regia (flamboyant)	*Tarchonanthus camphoratus*
Ficus microcarpa nitida (Indian laurel)	*Tibouchina spp.* (glory bush tree)
F. natalensis (Natal fig)	*Virgilia divaricata* (keurboom)

RIGHT *With the sea not far away, this truly beautiful garden was created on the Western Cape coast. Loads of good soil, compost and fertilizer were worked into the beds backed with phormiums, palms strelitzias and other plants which could stand up to the wind to shield the roses, perennials and annuals which were to come.*

OPPOSITE PAGE *Discounting sea breezes and salt air the owners planted a garden of annuals on the cliff top, their radiant colour having the perfect backdrop of the blue sea. Just below, coastal shrubs, including brachylaena and a golden bougainvillea, were planted to break the force of the wind.*

A natural windbreak consisting of a row, or better, two rows of shrubs on the sea-facing boundary will filter the wind. These will have to be very tough to stand up to their front-line situation. Then taller shrubs and trees can be planted behind them forming layers to reduce wind velocity. Ensure that you plant these close together to achieve density, which also cools the ground beneath them. Plant them when small so that their root systems can develop in their home soil, protecting them with windbreak netting at first if necessary.

Naturally, if there is a prevailing wind coming from one direction you will be able to plan your planting accordingly. It may sound a little tedious, but it really is worthwhile hosing down that hedge after extremely heavy winds have brought in salt-laden air.

ADAPTED PLANTS

It is well worthwhile giving thought to the indigenous plants growing in your coastal area. The coast silver oak *(Brachylaena discolor)* will grow on the dunes and is ideal for screening in coastal gardens. The crane flower *(Strelitzia reginae)* is native to the eastern Cape and will grace coastal gardens in this

SHRUBS AND CLIMBERS FOR COASTAL GARDENS

NATAL AND EAST COAST
Acalypha spp. (acalypha)
Allamanda cathartica
Breynia disticha 'Rosea-picta'
Mussaenda 'Alicia Luce' (flag bush)

NATAL, EASTERN & SOUTHERN CAPE
Burchellia bubalina
Ixora spp. (flame of the woods)

WESTERN CAPE
Berzelia lanuginosa (kolkol)
Brunia neglecta
Didelta carnosa

ALL AREAS
Bougainvillea hybrids
Brassaia actinophylla

Brunfelsia spp.
Buddleja auriculata
B. salviifolia
Callistemon citrinus
Carissa macrocarpa (amatungulu)
Cassia corymbosa (autumn cassia)
Cestrum nocturnum
Chrysanthemoides spp.
Cistus incanus (rock rose)
Coleonema spp. (confetti bush)
Coprosma repens (mirror plant)
Cotoneaster dammeri
C. horizontalis
Cunonia capensis (red alder)
Cuphea micropetala (tartan bush)
Dichorisandra thyrsiflora
   (blue-flowering reed)
Dieffenbachia picta

Echium fastuosum (pride of Madeira)
Erica spp. (heath)
Erythrina caffra (coral tree)
Euonymus japonicus
Euphorbia pulcherrima (poinsettia)
Euryops pectinatus
Grevillea hybrids
Hebe speciosa (veronica)
Hibiscus rosa-sinensis
Holmskioldia sanguinea
H. tettensis (wild parasol flower)
Hydrangea macrophylla
Justicia brandegeana (shrimp flower)
Lagerstroemia indica (pride of India)
Myrtus communis (common myrtle)
Nandina domestica (sacred bamboo)
Petrea volubilis (purple wreath)
Philodendron selloum

Plectranthus spp. (spur flower)
Plumeria rubra (frangipani)
Protea spp.
Pseuderanthemum alatum
Pyrostegia venusta (golden shower)
Quisqualis indica (Rangoon creeper)
Rhaphiolepis indica (Indian hawthorn)
Rhus spp.
Russelia equisetiformis (coral bush)
Schefflera arboricola (Hawaiian elf)
Solanum wendlandii (potato creeper)
Strelitzia reginae (crane flower)
S. nicolai (Natal wild banana)
Strongylodon macrobotrys (jade vine)
Tecoma capensis (Cape honeysuckle)
Tetrapanax papyrifer
Tibouchina spp. (glory bush)
Yucca filamentosa (Adam's needle)

region, while the bush violet *(Barleria obtusa)* will grow in almost any coastal garden. Then there are the hardy milkwood trees and the giant euphorbias.

There is a wonderful selection of dramatic-looking tropical plants, from the tall *Strelitzia nicolai* (Natal wild banana) and all kinds of leafy plants such as philodendrons and dieffenbachia, to crotons and acalyphas which need sun.

Cassia corymbosa makes a good hedge and many common garden plants will do well protected from the salt wind behind just such a hedge.

Grass grows well in the humid coastal air. As an expanse of lawn is always cooling and good to walk on after the heat of beach sand, find out which grass is best for your area. This will definitely vary depending on prevalent climatic conditions.

Note that *Metrosideros tomentosa* (New Zealand Christmas tree) – which grows so well in the Western Cape and which many coastal gardeners have found to be one of very few worthwhile wind-resistant plants – is now a declared invader. It is in Category 3, which means that you are no longer allowed to plant it, although you are allowed to keep it if it is already growing in your garden.

ANNUALS FOR COASTAL GARDENS

Amaranthus caudatus (love-lies-bleeding)
Anchusa capensis (Cape forget-me-not)
Anigozanthos flavidus (kangaroo paw)
Celosia argentea (garden cockscomb)
Coleus x hybrids
Dimorphotheca spp. (Namaqualand daisy)
Dorotheanthus bellidiformis (Bokbaai vygie)
Gaillardia pulchella (Indian blanket)
Gomphrena globosa (globe amaranth)
Helianthus annuus (common sunflower)

Impatiens spp.
Lavatera trimestris (mallow)
Lobularia maritima (alyssum)
Salvia leucantha (Mexican sage)
S. splendens (scarlet sage)
Tagetes erecta (African marigold)
Torenia fournieri (blue wings)
Tropaeolum majus (nasturtium)
Ursinia spp.
Zinnia elegans (zinnia)

PERENNIALS FOR COASTAL GARDENS

WESTERN CAPE

Agathosma ciliarus (buchu)
Aloe distans (Saldanha aloe)
A. striata (coral aloe)
Arctotheca populifolia (sand daisy)
Arctotis acaulis (marigold)
Aristea major (tall aristea)
Asparagus aethiopicus (haakdoring)
Chasmanthe floribunda
Pelargonium spp.
Plectranthus spp.
Scabiosa spp.

NATAL/SUB-TROPICAL

Aechma fasciata (urn plant)
Aglaonema spp.
Anthurium spp. (flamingo flower)
Aphelandra squarrosa 'Louisae'

Asparagus densiflorus
Billbergia spp. (bromeliad)
Caladium bicolor
Calathea spp.
Cordyline spp.
Cyrtanthus mackenii (ifafa lily)
Streptocarpus spp.

ALL AREAS

Acanthus mollis (bear's breeches)
Achillea millefolium hybrids (yarrow)
Agapanthus spp.
Agave spp.
Ajuga reptans (carpet bugle)
Alocasia spp. (elephant's ear)
Aloe arborescens (krans aloe)
A. ferox (Cape aloe)
Alstroemeria spp. (Inca lily)

Aster novi-belgii (Michaelmas daisy)
Barleria obtusa (bush violet)
Bulbine frutescens (stalked bulbine)
Canna flaccida
Carpobrotus edulis (sour fig)
Centaurea cineraria (dusty miller)
Chamaemelum nobile (chamomile)
Chlorophytum comosum
Chondropetalum tectorum
Convolvulus sabatius
Cotyledon orbiculata
Crassula spp.
Crocosmia aurea (montbretia)
Diascia integerrima (twinspur)
Drosanthemum speciosum (vygie)
Echeveria spp.
Elegia capensis (broom reed)
Erigeron karvinskianus (fleabane)

Felicia amelloides (blue marguerite)
Gazania spp.
Geranium incanum
G. sanguineum (crane bill)
Gerbera jamesonii (Barberton daisy)
Gloriosa superba (flame lily)
Hedera spp. (ivy)
Hemerocallis spp. (day lily)
Indigofera procumbens (indigo)
Lavandula spp. (lavender)
Irisine lindenii (blood leaf)
Leucadendron spp.
Limonium spp. (sea lavender/statice)
Nerine spp.
Osteospermum ecklonis (river daisy)
Physostegia virginiana
Pilea cadierei (aluminium plant)
Syngonium podophyllum

Hot and dry areas

A sun-dried area or stony outcrop may be difficult to plant, but there are a number of things that can be done by way of improving the soil, garden design, choosing the right plants, and providing protection of various kinds for your plants. (*See waterwise gardening on pages 156 – 158.*)

IMPROVE SOIL

Before considering what to plant, the first thing to do is to improve the soil. Adding compost and other organic material in vast quantities will without doubt not only improve the fertility of the soil, but also its ability to retain water.

Soil improvers, such as gypsum or lime to break up hard-packed soil, or water-retaining gel around those very special plants, may be necessary.

USE WATER EFFECTIVELY

Using mulch all over your garden — in the form of organic material or even pebbles, chipped bark or a drought-resistant ground cover — will conserve moisture and reduce ground temperature. Water is best applied at the base of plants during the coolest time of day. Drip irrigation to each really needy plant is the best under these circumstances and it is surprisingly economical with water.

GARDEN DESIGN

If your whole garden is hot and dry, it is a good idea to keep your lawn as small as possible as it is a big water consumer. Erect a pergola and trellis around your patio and plant these with creepers for shade and a windbreak. A hot, dry slope can be transformed by turning it into a rock garden

PLANTS SUITABLE FOR HOT, DRY AREAS

TREES

Acacia spp. (acacia)
Buddleja saligna (false olive)
Cussonia spp. (cabbage tree)
Olea europaea africana (wild olive)
Olea europaea africana (wild olive)
Pappea capensis
Plumeria spp. (frangipani)
Rhus spp. (karee)
Tarchonanthus camphoratus
Ziziphus mucronata (buffalo thorn)

SHRUBS

Aloe spp.
Barleria obtusa (bush violet)

Bauhinia galpinii (pride-of-de-Kaap)
Bougainvillea hybrids
Carissa bispinosa (hedge thorn)
Chaenomeles spp. (quince)
Cistus hybrids (rock rose)
Euphorbia spp.
Lagerstroemia indica (pride of India)
Lavandula spp. (lavender)
Leonotis leonurus (wild dagga)
Melaleuca spp.
Nandina domestica (sacred bamboo)
Plumbago auriculata
Rosmarinus officinalis (rosemary)
Sedum acre (stonecrop)
Tecoma capensis (Cape honeysuckle)

Yucca spp.

PERENNIALS

Achillea millefolium (yarrow)
Agapanthus spp.
Agave americana (century plant)
A. attenuata (dragon tree)
Arctotheca populifolia (sand daisy)
Anigozanthus flavidus
Cotyledon orbiculata
Crassula spp.
Dietes spp.
Furcraea foetida (Mauritius hemp)
Kalanchoe tubiflora
Kniphofia x praecox (red-hot poker)
Limonium spp. (statice)

Oenothera speciosa 'Rosea'
Stapelia spp. (carrion flower)
Strelitzia reginae (crane flower)

GROUND COVERS

Aptenia cordifolia (heartleaf)
Arctotis hybrids
Carpobrotus edulis (sour fig)
Drosanthemum speciosum
Echeveria spp.
Gazania spp.
Lampranthus spp. (vygies)
Osteospermum ecklonis (river daisy)
Othona carnosa
Verbena spp.

(see pages 118 – 121). If the rocks are well placed they will create shade for smaller plants, while the roots of larger perennials will be happy to creep under the rocks for protection.

Probably the first plants to come to mind for a rock garden are the succulents and cacti, which are able to store water in their leaves and stems for future use, and indeed there is a wealth of them to choose from. Think of the low-growing mesembryanthemums, the lampranthus and others, which will send out their stems and succulent leaves, then produce an abundance of brilliant flowers. Then there are kalanchoes and aloes, the small ones and the giants like the candelabra. A rock garden in the hot, dry air can be spectacular, but perhaps too seasonal for most gardeners.

CREATE A WINDBREAK

Plant a group of trees or shrubs to form a natural windbreak and bring welcome shade. Give them a good start by planting them in sizeable holes filled with topsoil, plenty of organic material, superphosphate and bonemeal. Make a basin around each one to hold water and cover this with a good mulch. You can protect your group of saplings from hot, drying winds with special nylon windbreak netting while they establish themselves.

Choose those trees which are used to such harsh conditions, preferably with a tap root which will find its way deep down into the soil. Consider indigenous trees and shrubs which are used to fending for themselves, bearing in mind that many of them grow very large. They will need loving care for the first year or two. Acacias, or thorn trees, once established, will not need much more attention. *Acacia sieberiana*, the paperbark acacia, has a lovely spreading habit.

The shrub, *Bauhinia galpinii* (pride-of-de-Kaap), with its rambling growth and brick-red flowers, can take light frost. *Buddleja saligna* is a small slender tree, drought-resistant and hardy to frost, as are the wild olive and many others. *Buddleja salviifolia* (sage-leafed buddleja) and *B. pulchella* can also withstand drought conditions.

It is wise to ask your local garden centre which trees and shrubs do best in your area.

ANNUALS AND PERENNIALS

If your hot and dry area is level, it can be made more viable by first improving the soil's water retention and optimizing your use of water. With this done, you will be surprised to see what a range of plants will do well. Annuals may look fragile, but, given good soil and water, they will thrive willingly. Try zinnias, marigolds, salvias and verbenas. From the indigenous annuals, include ursinia, arctotis and Namaqualand daisies (*Dimorphotheca aurantiaca*).

Seeds of these can be scattered liberally, covered with compost and sand and watered very gently, then kept damp at all times. Perennials which do not mind the hot sun are the gazanias, Barberton daisies (*Gerbera jamesonii*), lavender, rosemary, thyme and everlastings (*Helichrysum bracteatum*).

There are ground covers which will form a green carpet under hot and dry conditions, the best one being heartleaf (*Aptenia cordifolia*), with its low spread of small succulent leaves.

In general, look out for plants with succulent leaves; grey or blueish foliage; thorns; leaves reduced in size, tough, leathery or hairy; thick, fleshy roots or thick corky bark. These have made adaptations to their environment and will usually cope well.

OPPOSITE PAGE
Seeming to up hold their arms in supplication, Pachypodium namaquanum (half-mens) make a statement in any garden. They can withstand dry conditions, but are frost tender. Their stems are covered with thorns and their leaves are minimal, leaving them looking stark and dramatic amid a sea of pebbles.

BELOW *Salvia leucantha is an old favourite, valued for its ability to stand up to dry conditions. It can be cut back hard after flowering, and overcrowded plantings can be thinned out by taking out the entire clump and dividing it.*

A damp area

It is difficult to believe that any area which is permanently damp can be considered a problem in a country where water is so precious. We probably regard those with a low-lying, damp patch as fortunate indeed. But it may bring its problems of oxygen-starved soil, inaccessibility and smell.

TRY TO DIVERT WATER

Ascertain where the water comes from. Ensure that it is not polluted. If it is, contact your local authority.

If it is general seepage, you may need to install some drainage. You might also try digging holes down into the damp area and sinking half drums with holes in their sides and bottom, so that water can seep in. This will create pools where you can plant water plants.

TACKLE THE SOIL

Dig organic matter into the soil as it will absorb water and also improve soil texture so that oxygen is allowed in. With the right equipment you could also fill up dips in the garden.

You could also change levels in other ways like making a raised bed and filling it with well-prepared soil which will then drain freely.

PLANTING SUGGESTIONS

Tree ferns and low-growing ferns are ideal, as are reeds which will help absorb water. Candelabra primulas and graceful arum lilies love damp conditions. The Louisiana (or swamp) irises and *Iris pseudacorus* (the yellow flag) will grow in or near the water, while *I. kaempferi* and *I. sibirica* will grow at the edge of the water.

Gunnera, with its huge umbrella of leaves will need water during spring and summer. It dies down in winter.

Water lilies and waterblommetjies will grow in water which is at least half a metre in depth. Do not be tempted to plant water lettuce or Kariba weed in the water. Both are declared aliens. At the edge of the damp spot, try a ground cover of ajuga.

There are few shrubs and trees which will tolerate airless, water-logged soil, but sufficiently far from the really wet soil you could safely plant *Acer spp.* (maples), which can be small upright trees or have a weeping form, tall *Cyperus papyrus* or even the smaller dwarf papyrus, which will grow fast. Day lilies and hostas will look good at the margins. Astilbes (goat's beard) are delightful plants which enjoy the water. They have slender stems and bear plumes of white or pink flowers.

Blood root *(Wachendorfia thyrsiflora)* is an indigenous plant which loves damp, peat-like soil. It carries tall spikes of yellow flowers from early spring and onwards into early summer.

A steep slope

Apart from the danger of loss of soil in heavy rain, a slope can present difficulties of access and plants may find it difficult to obtain a grip on the soil.

PLANTING SOLUTIONS

Large cascading plants can form a mat of vegetation which will break the fall of rain as well as bind the soil. Bougainvilleas, plumbago, *Bauhinia galpinii* (pride-of-de-Kaap) are some examples. *Coprosma x kirkii* will also be most useful. Place these in substantial, well-prepared planting holes at the top of the slope or, if the slope is long, at the top and halfway

BELOW *A steep slope linking the level area near the house to the lower section of the garden did not deter this gardener, who made the most of it by constructing two flights of steps and a waterfall. Then a lush grove was created, using rocks of various shapes and sizes, with pockets large enough to accept tree ferns, phormiums, cordylines, crotons (codiaeums), dwarf bamboos, ferns and other suitable plants.*

down. As soon as they are growing strongly, pinch back the growth to help produce many stems to spread out over the surface of the slope.

Other plants which will bind the soil and cushion the effect of a downpour are the ivies. Agapanthus, day lilies, mondo grass and, for very hot parts, gazanias, arctotis, erigeron, osteospermum, crassulas and other creeping succulents will also stabilize a slope.

OTHER SOLUTIONS

A rock garden could be the answer (see pages 119 – 121) or you could construct terraces. Retain any topsoil you remove in the process and fill up your terraces with this soil.

A drain can be dug across the slope and filled with pebbles, to break the run of the water and lead it away. Logs, too, can be laid across a slope, with plants inserted behind them. If you are making steps to lead up the slope, start at the bottom and work your way upwards.

To support a high bank, or an unstable sandy bank, curved, hollow concrete blocks could be the answer. These blocks are laid with each half overlapping the one beneath, then they are filled with soil.

Plants can be placed in the soil, which makes for an attractive as well as sturdy construction. These blocks can also be used for terraces. A wall of used tyres will serve the same purpose.

Unsightly structures

Even a well-built garage or garden shed can distract from the overall effect of the garden. A swimming-pool pump is a necessary evil, and manhole covers and downpipes cannot be wished away.

PLANTING SOLUTIONS

A solution is to either cover a shed with creepers, or to screen it off by means of a wall or hedge. You can train rambling roses or ivy over a garden shed for a charming, old-world look.

However, it is probably most practical to divide the garage and the parking area off from the main garden by means of good hedges or wooden fences which are then either covered with creepers or hid-

den by shrubs and trees. If this is done, then a door or gate must be erected, to define the entrance to the garden.

CONTAINERS

Manhole covers are unsightly and the best way to disguise them is to place large containers on them. Do not make these so large that they are impossible to move. A decorative wheelbarrow filled with plants is easy to move and will be large enough to cover the manhole.

You could also train a ground cover over a manhole cover, as long as it does not have invasive roots. However if the plumber comes to inspect the drains, you will have to start over again.

OTHER SOLUTIONS

A swimming-pool pump is not a thing of beauty. A cover of fibreglass or similar material with a natural rock finish will disguise the pump, otherwise plants can be placed around it, preferably those with shallow root systems, such as phormiums and ferns.

A downpipe in a prominent position on the house wall can be disguised with a cladding of trellis and an attractive, but non-invasive small climbing plant. Alternatively a cage of small-gauge chicken wire can be fixed around the pipe and the climber trained up this.

ABOVE *Gloriously variegated foliage plants both cover the structure and brighten the shadows. Lamiums cover the ground, while ivy covers the shed. To crown it all a hellebore displays its unusual pale green flowers.*

Care & maintenance

Through the year your garden needs loving attention, with a watchful eye kept by a gardener attuned to the seasons. By getting a little closer to your garden and plants you will see instinctively what their needs are. Some tasks come only at certain times, as do seasons of blooming, of growing, of resting, each with its special needs. This section offers guidelines for the major areas of garden care, starting with a round-up of the seasons, reminding you of special tasks that come up as your garden follows its cycle of growth and rest, through spring, summer, autumn and winter.

The thatched roof is an ideal backdrop for the profusion of flowers which have been brought together, each of them in supreme good health and each given its own space, yet contributing to the lovely overall picture. Petunias and lobelias in a pot are framed by the spring-green of the grape vine, creating a delicate cameo, while the roses, in an assortment of standard, ground-cover, bush and miniature forms, with Lysimachia nummularia (creeping Jenny) between, are more demanding of attention.

Year-round care

To keep your garden and plants in the best possible condition, you need to perform certain maintenance tasks such as weeding, feeding and dead-heading regularly. Exactly what needs to be done will to a certain degree depend on the plants in your garden. This seasonal approach will give you very general guidelines. For specific plant maintenance, you may have to consult a comprehensive plant-reference manual.

Spring

The first day of September is the start of spring, but even before that you will feel a renewal of spirit, a new determination to do wonderful things in your garden. The exuberance of the season is infectious, for this is the time of new growth, of warmth spreading through the soil, of stirrings underground, of buds bursting joyfully into a new world. Rather than a delicate nymph, surely spring should remind us of a happy giant, healthy, bountiful and strong.

Spend a little time each day simply walking in the garden. Rejoice in the sweet scent of jasmine and hyacinths, marvel at the industriousness of the bees and the endearing faces of the pansies as they lift them to the life-giving sun. Then take a notebook and write down what should have been done, what looks utterly lovely and should be repeated, and which tasks lie ahead for summer. Then it's to work.

Spraying season

Choose pesticides from the vast range of enviro-friendly products available. When spraying for fungi, cover the entire plant and the surrounding soil. If equipment is used for both pesticides and foliar fertilizing, thoroughly clean it between applications – a small amount of herbicide could have a devastating effect on healthy plants. Wear protective clothing and wash these and any exposed parts of the body after spraying. Keep the labels on garden chemicals legible and destroy empty containers so that they

cannot be used for other purposes. Look out for beetles and their creamy white larvae in the soil. If possible remove them and drown them in hot, salty water, otherwise spray them.

Care for annuals

Remove winter-flowering annuals like *Primula malacoides* if they have come to the end of their blooming period. Annuals showing their first flowers should have those first buds pinched out. This will induce them to produce many more flowers.

Many flowers will be in full bloom, looking colourful and healthy. Take off any dead flowers immediately, otherwise the plant will think it has done its job and start to make seeds. Give annuals a dressing of general fertilizer and regular, deep watering.

If you want to keep some special seed, then certainly allow one or two plants to go to seed. Collect it on a warm, dry day, making sure that the seed is dry, then pack it into paper packets or bottles, add a little fungicide and a label with the name and date.

As you take out spent annuals and put them on the compost heap, so the soil must be replenished. Dig it over to aerate it, add compost and 2:3:2 and leave it for a week or two.

Planting new seedlings

Choose from the punnets of seedlings and seed packets and plan wonderful colour schemes of annuals alone, as well as a mixture of annuals and perennials. Where summer colour is concerned, you can choose plants for cool tranquility or an exciting, vibrant effect. Be brave and try something new.

When you plant the next crop of seedlings, mix a dessertspoon of superphosphate into the bottom of each hole. From now on, new plants should never be allowed to dry out completely. Protect them from hot, drying wind by watering them well and covering them with floating anti-frost fabric.

BULBS

Some of your bulbous flowering plants may be past their prime, having enjoyed the cold winter weather. If you want them to do their best next year, feed and water them now, keeping the leaves strong and healthy to feed the bulbs. If you think the leaves look untidy, twist them together and lay them down along the soil's surface. When they have turned yellow, cut them down to the ground. Some bulbs can be lifted. Indigenous bulbs from the winter-rainfall areas will not cope well with summer downpours and should be lifted and kept in a cool, dry place. Some, like

sparaxis, set seed readily and the seeds can be collected and stored for later use.

Plant summer bulbs such as dahlias now if you have not yet done so. Summer bulbs already in the ground will need an extra layer of mulch, plus, when they are producing leaves, a dose of liquid manure and another mulch. As this is the start of the iris season, visit a specialist nursery and make your choice from the incredible range.

SHRUBS

Some shrubs may have been hit hard by frost, leaving them looking sad and bedraggled. If you are sure there is no more frost to come, cut these shrubs back to healthy growth.

Summer-flowering shrubs will need extra food and water for the new season. Lightly dig the soil around hydrangeas, then give them a dressing of fertilizer, followed by a thorough soaking and a good, thick layer of mulch.

Fuchsias will start to produce new shoots. As soon as there are four pairs of leaves on a shoot, pinch back its end to encourage the development of more stems. Flowers bloom on new growth, so help your plants produce as many stems as possible with this pinching-back method. Give them a high-nitrogen fertilizer early in the season, adding phosphorus and potassium when foliage has developed.

TREES

Blossom trees make the transition from winter into spring with a flourish. If they are to be trimmed or shaped, this should be done as soon as flowering is over. This applies to azaleas and camellias as well. Although they don't usually need cutting back, they will need a good thick mulch of pine needles, pine bark or compost.

LAWN

Set your mower to a low cut and trim the grass almost to the ground. Scarify it and take away the clippings. Give it a dressing of 2:3:2 followed by a thorough soaking. If you are short of water, use slow-release fertilizer.

BELOW *It's early spring in a Johannesburg garden where clear pink tulips stand tiptoe on their Persian carpet of richly coloured* Primula acaulis. *Behind them a cloud of* Primula malacoides *hover misty and mauve. Tulips, treated to take our conditions, are available in May. They should be planted immediately after buying.*

LEFT *Sweet Williams* (Dianthus barbatus) *should be in every spring garden. These generous bloomers come in a huge diversity of colours and colour combinations. Their flowers last long on the plant and they make gorgeous cut flowers. They like lime in the soil, and a position which receives sun for most of the day.*

The lawn may be suffering from last summer's family cricket matches and winter's soccer games. If so, dig over the bare patches, plant new grass and give it a dressing of compost and sand. Cover these areas with twigs to prevent footsteps from causing more damage. You may find that there is a definite trail of worn grass traced across the lawn, which signals the need for a path of flagstones or other material. For those heavily shaded parts, sow the seed of Shade-Over grass (see page 55).

ROSES

Roses can be given a handful of 2:3:2, their first feed since pruning, followed by 3:1:5 for good quality flowers. Water them well and mulch. Keep a sharp lookout for black spot and mildew. Prevention is better than cure, so start a programme of preventive spraying now. Cut banksia roses back hard after flowering, removing untidy, dead-wood growth.

PREPARE FOR SUMMER RAINS

If you garden in a summer rainfall area, prepare for the rain by making sure that any surplus water can escape from the garden. Clear drains, dig shallow furrows across steep paths and cut back overhanging branches which could become heavy with water and break.

CLIMBERS

Check that their supports are strong enough for the new heavy foliage to come. The flowered stems of bougainvilleas, which have given generously of their brilliant colours, can now be cut back hard. Then apply a dressing of 2:3:2 and water it in well to encourage healthy foliage. When buds first appear,

PLANTING FOR SUMMER

BULBS & BULBOUS PLANTS

Agapanthus spp.
Alstroemeria aurea (Inca lily)
Begonia hybrids
Canna indica hybrids
Crinum spp.
Dahlia hybrids
Dierama pendulum (harebell)
Eucomis autumnalis (pineapple flower)
Galtonia candicans (berg lily)
Gladiolus hybrids
Gloriosa superba (flame lily)
Hemerocallis hybrids (day lily)
Iris fulva (Louisiana iris)
I. kaempferi (Japanese iris)
Kniphofia praecox (red-hot poker)
Liatris pycnostachya (gay feather)
Lilium spp.

Nerine sarniensis (Guernsey lily)
Schizostylis coccinea (river lily)
Tigridia pavonia (tiger flower)
Watsonia spp.
Zantedeschia aethiopica (arum lily)

SUMMER-FLOWERING SHRUBS

Abelia x grandiflora (glossy abelia)
Gardenia spp.
Hibiscus rosa-sinensis varieties
Hydrangea macrophylla hybrids
   (Christmas flower)
Murraya exotica (orange jasmine)
Plumbago auriculata (blue plumbago)
P. auriculata 'Alba' (white plumbago)
Solanum rantonnettii (blue potato bush)
Tecoma stans
Tibouchina spp. (glory bush/tree)

PLANTING FOR SUMMER

PERENNIALS

Astilbe x arendsii (goat's beard)
Chrysanthemum maximum (shasta daisy)
Dietes grandiflora (wild iris)
Gaura lindheimeri
Monarda didyma (bergamot)
Phlox paniculata (perennial phlox)
Physostegia virginiana (obedience plant)
Rehmannia angulata (Chinese foxglove)
Thalictrum delavayi (meadow rue)

ANNUALS

Acroclinium roseum (everlasting)
Ageratum houstonianum (floss flower)
Alcea rosea (hollyhock)
Amaranthus tricolor (Joseph's coat)
Ammi majus (Queen Anne's lace)
Anchusa spp. (forget-me-not)

Browallia speciosa (sapphire flower)
Callistephus chinensis (Chinese aster)
Chrysanthemum paludosum (annual chrysanthemum)
Cleome spinosa (spider flower)
Coleus hybrids (flame nettle)
Coreopsis tinctoria (tickweed)
Dahlia hybrids
Gaillardia pulchella (Indian blanket)
Gomphrena globosa (bachelor's button)
Gourd (ornamental)
Helianthus annuus (common sunflower)
Helichrysum bracteatum (everlasting)
Iberis umbellata (candytuft)
Impatiens balsamina (garden balsam)
Impatiens walleriana (busy Lizzie)
Kochia scoparia 'Trichophylla' (burning bush)

Linaria maroccana (toad flax)
Lobelia erinus
Lobularia maritima (alyssum)
Matricaria eximia (feverfew)
Nicotiana alata (tobacco plant)
Penstemon spectabilis
Phlox drummondii (annual phlox)
Primula malacoides (fairy primrose)
Rudbeckia hirta (gloriosa daisy)
Salpiglossis sinuata (painted tongue)
Salvia spp.
Tagetes erecta (marigold)
Torenia fournieri (blue wings)
Tropaeolum majus (nasturtium)
Verbascum phoeniceum (purple mullein)
Verbena hybrids (garden verbena)
Xeranthemum annuum (immortelle)
Zinnia elegans

BELOW *Forsythia can take heavy frost, and does not mind if it is not watered regularly. Yet in spring it is transformed into a gleaming extravagance of gold with a multitude of yellow flowers carried on the bare and slender stems.*

cut right back on water. Trim back petreas and the larger, more showy hybrids of clematis.

PERENNIALS

In the mixed border there are probably clumps of perennials which have slept through winter. If these need to be divided, lift the entire clump, separate the plants, throw away the inner spent part and replant the outer growth into good enriched soil.

Get rid of woody growth in patches of ground cover by forking around and through the clumps. Drench with water and give a dressing of compost. Consider digging out and replanting patches of really old growth.

PLANT FOR SUMMER

Share your garden with friends and neighbours. Softwood cuttings can be taken of most plants at this time of year (see page 163). In the colder gardens there may still be a danger of frost – delay any new planting until frost is definitely over. Position fine net bags to catch the seeds of hellebores as the pods ready themselves to burst. Replenish the soil in borders with 2:3:2 and compost. Choose summer-flowering plants from the lists on pages 143 and 144.

Summer

Summer means balmy evenings, walking barefoot on the lawn with the trees rolling out full, black shadows before them, the scent of lilies, lavender and summer roses, the fun of holidays and festivities.

Janus, the god after whom January was named, is often shown with two profiles, one looking forward, one looking back. This is highly relevant at this time – we can look back on the festival of colour which has already taken place in the garden, and forward to just as much glorious colour, and more, staying with us for some months to come.

ANNUALS

All the seedlings planted in spring will have come to wonderful bloom. Plant more quick growers such as alyssum, portulaca, nasturtiums, sunflowers, marigolds, salvias, ageratums and zinnias in early summer to grace the garden while the weather is still warm.

Plant beans, parsnips, carrots, turnips, radishes and beets. In February you can still plant coleus, amaranthus, gaillardia and celosia for late-summer colour in warmer gardens, as well as strawberry runners in summer-rainfall areas. Prepare trenches for sweet peas: dig down 60 cm, loosen the soil at the bottom and fill the trench with a mixture of compost and good garden soil, with some bone-meal and superphosphate. Keep up your routine of dead-heading to keep annuals in bloom.

BULBOUS PLANTS

Dahlias are proudly bearing their bountiful crop of flowers. These worthwhile plants can be tall and gangling, or compact. The pompons have very neat flowers on slender stems. Remove side buds, leaving one terminal bud. Stake the taller plants well and soak thoroughly. Remove spent flowers which may look untidy as their lower petals turn brown.

LEFT *Pride of India, Lagerstroemia indica, has been with us for a long time, but now colours have been enriched, and there are dwarf varieties for small gardens. They bloom at the height of summer, and some towns have planted them as street trees to create their own festival of colour. Their glowing autumn leaves are an added asset.*

Liliums are a wonderfully perfumed part of summer. When you pick them try not to take too much stem, as the leaves are necessary for the health of the plant. If you need to transport them, clip off the stamens, as they are covered with pollen which will stain clothing and adjacent petals. Pick them when they are just about to open, then wrap each bloom in toilet tissue, gently tied up with wool. Some liliums will have finished blooming. Give them weekly applications of liquid seaweed fertilizer to feed the leaves and thus the bulbs. Before the leaves die down, mark the spot where they are planted. Tiger lilies bloom in February and will need food and water.

Agapanthus, ranging from giants to charming miniatures, are welcome in the summer garden. Divide them into smaller clumps if they are over-crowded.

Lift and divide irises and arum lilies when they have finished flowering in late summer, and plant lachenalia and nerine bulbs.

You can sow seeds of ranunculus and anemones during December and January. After sowing, keep the trays damp in the cool shade. When the seedlings are easy to handle, prick them out and keep them damp. As they grow, feed them with weak liquid manure the colour of weak tea.

FAVOURITE FRAGRANCES

Frangipani and gardenias, with their heady, heavy fragrance, are veritable *parfumeries* of summer. Gather a harvest of frangipani blossoms and float them in a bowl of water for a lovely dinner-table centrepiece. Take cuttings of your favourite frangipani now, but don't get that milky substance on your hands as it will irritate your skin.

LAWN

Water regularly, especially in winter-rainfall areas, and remove weeds promptly. Your lawn may need more frequent mowing, but keep to your regular feeding programme. Towards the end of summer, dress lawns with 2:3:2 or 3:1:5 (which is high in potassium) to strengthen them before winter.

ROSES

Regularly cut back the stems of flowered roses about halfway down, and give them plenty of water in the winter-rainfall areas.

The plants can have a summer pruning in January. Take out all unwanted stems, then cut back flowered stems by about a third. Watch closely for any sign of red spider during hot weather (also on other plants) and spray regularly.

Rambling roses which have finished flowering should be cut back hard, fed and watered.

TRIMMING AND TIDYING

Chrysanthemums will have tall, strong stems by now. If you are brave enough, cut these down to half their height in mid-December, which will make for more flower stems in autumn. In the hot months, growth will be tremendous, especially where humidity is high. The judicious cutting back of shrubs will tidy them up and encourage new, healthy growth.

Cut poinsettias back to at least half their size in February, so that there will be more stems, and thus more flowers, in winter. Take off any dead or unhealthy fern leaves with a clean cut.

GARDEN COMPETITIONS

Garden competitions are often held in January. If you haven't entered your garden, take time to visit the prize-winning gardens to see what you can learn. If you have entered your garden, make sure everything is neat and tidy before the judges arrive. Mow the lawn one or even two days before the time to ensure that no unsightly marks are left, and trim the edges. Take off every dead flower head. Put all the tools away, sweep the paths, leave glasses and cool drinks for the judges, then keep out of their way.

Coleus are annuals which bear leaves in a multitude of colours and colour variations. To keep them producing those colourful leaves, don't allow them to bloom – nip out the flower buds as they appear.

Take cuttings of shrubs, fairly woody, but of the present season's growth. Lavender is a good subject as it will grow fast. Take 10 cm long clematis cuttings, make a slit 2,5 cm from the base and plant this, burying the lower pair of leaves.

WATERING

On hot days, watering and the retention of water are of great importance. If your water supply is restricted, water only those plants which really need it, and mulch. Hydrangeas and astilbes need plenty of water and you should lay down mulch wherever you can. Ferns will need a lot of water both around their stems and as a fine spray on their leaves. Dig over hard-baked soil or any rainwater will just run off.

ABOVE *The Golden Shower* (Pyrostegia venusta) *is well named indeed, as its glittering orange flowers cascade down walls and arches. Thriving in the warm-climate garden, it can be seen during autumn and winter. It needs full sun and very well-drained soil.*

Autumn

The burnished richness of crimson, the sumptuous glory of purple and gold … your garden's colours proclaim that autumn is here. As deciduous plants feel their winter rest draw near, the goodness of the leaves flows back into the mother plant. Then a line of scar tissue forms across the base of each leaf and it loosens and falls. It settles on the earth in sun-soaked fulfilment to perform its last task – adding to the rich humus which will give back life in spring.

As the air and soil cool, growth will slow down, so don't expect too much of your plants at this time of the year. In the Western Cape, gardeners will look forward to the rain, while in the summer-rainfall areas the earth and air may be dry, so maintain a careful watering programme.

When planning your winter and spring garden, bear in mind that some of your trees are deciduous and will be bare of leaves in winter, letting the sun shine through for plants to grow beneath them.

ANNUALS

Self-sets may be making their appearance – tiny plants arising from those seeds left in the ground by last year's annuals such as primulas, silenes, heart-sease and forget-me-nots. Water them well, thin them out and plant them into good soil.

Buy generous packets of Namaqualand daisy (dimorphotheca) and ursinia seeds and sow them in every spot you can, even in pots. They will come up and bloom willingly if they are given water and a dressing of 2:3:2 when they have produced a good-

PROTECTION AGAINST FROST

Towards the end of autumn, early frost can be a menace. Give newly-planted shrubs protection in the form of hessian, cardboard boxes or plastic sheeting. Make sure that the plant does not touch the plastic, as the leaves could be burnt.

Shrubs which are frost-tender should not be cut back at this time, as the new tender growth will be badly affected by the frost. Any plants which have been damaged by frost should be left alone, and not have those burnt parts removed. Move frost-tender container-grown plants into a sheltered position.

---

ly supply of leaves. Find something new – colours, perhaps dwarf forms of old favourites. Work out colour schemes – all white with alyssum, candytuft, pansies, delphiniums; or a striking mix, with purple larkspurs and orange calendulas. Don't shy away from bright, bold colours. Look for vivid red ranunculus, crimson poppies, purple pansies.

Sow sweetpeas into the prepared trenches. When seedlings emerge, protect them from cutworms with cardboard collars. Remove side growth and keep well watered. Protect seedlings from birds by sprinkling them with a solution of 28 g of alum to five litres of water, or cover them with bird netting.

PERENNIALS

Anemone hupehensis (wind anemones) bloom in March. They will grow in shade, semi-shade or in a position which receives morning sun, and they do like a cool root run. Cut the flowered stems down to the ground and mulch.

Perennials can be divided in March and April, although some gardeners like to do this in spring. Some, including watsonias and agapanthus, don't like to be divided, and it is wise to plant out fairly large clumps, rather than separate plants.

There is a multitude of autumn-blooming plectranthus, from the tall fruticosus to the ground cover ambiguus. These indigenous plants are undemanding and there are species for sun and shade. If you don't have any in your garden, resolve to include them so they will be blooming generously next autumn. They can be cut down when flowering is over.

Physostegia virginiana (obedience plant) makes a good show, but can run wild. Remove a good proportion of the flowered plants otherwise they will take over their part of the garden completely. Those that remain will multiply in turn.

April is the time for chrysanthemums, with their typical autumn scent. Cut the flowered stems right down, and either divide the clumps or wait until spring, when the new shoots can be taken off and planted as cuttings.

LILIES

Day lilies will have an autumn blooming at the end of April and into May and will need to be given a feed of 2:3:2. Maintain deep, regular watering until the blooming period is over. Other liliums, such as the pink tiger lily (*Lilium speciosum*), also choose these months to bloom. They will appreciate weekly doses of weak liquid manure and a good mulch. You will find that orange tiger lilies have small black bulbils in their leaf axils, which can be removed and planted on the surface of moist sand (*see page 164*).

New lilium bulbs will be available for March planting on a bed of sand in well-drained soil enriched with organic material, superphosphate and bonemeal. Mark the spot and as soon as growth is evident, feed every 10 days with liquid fertilizer. Keep them damp from the time of planting.

SUMMER-FLOWERING BULBS

Summer-flowering bulbs will be getting ready for their winter rest and can be left to their own devices. Dahlias will die down before winter. After the last leaf has faded cut the stems right down, lift each clump, label it and store it in a dry place. If you decide to leave your dahlias in the soil, push a stick bearing a label into the soil beside each clump.

ORANGE AND RED
Prepare to warm up the winter garden with the glow of red. You'll find it in aloes galore, poinsettias (in pots on the patio in frosty areas), the Natal bottlebrush (*Greyia sutherlandii*), bougainvilleas, succulents, the coast coral tree (*Erythrina caffra*), the common coral tree (*Erythrina lysistemon*), red flowering cherry trees and red ranunculus.

For a splash of orange try golden shower (*Pyrostegia venusta*), which is frost-tender but will still be blooming in the warmer areas), leonotis, red-hot pokers, gazanias, *Watsonia meriana*, the parasol flower (*Holmskioldia sanguinea*), *Strelitzia reginae*, flowering pomegranate and nasturtiums.

BELOW *Red-hot pokers (Kniphofia praecox) are our indigenous flaming torches which grow in fields, and some even in damp patches, blooming for the most part in autumn and winter. Here they are in the company of orange Crocosmia in March.*

WINTER AND SPRING BULBS

Now is the time to plant those lovely bulbs that will brighten up beds and borders in late winter and spring. They look equally good in pots and also mix well with annuals. If you are going to combine annuals with bulbs, you could sow seed of linaria, alyssum or virginia stocks in March, then plant the bulbs between them at bulb-planting time in April. Always get your annual seedlings going first, then put in the bulbs so that the bulbs are not damaged.

Daffodils combine well with mauve alyssum, nemophila, myosotis, lobelia and primulas. Try hyacinths with Dutch irises and plant a pot with muscari and lachenalias. Group chincherinchees close together and surround them with *Bellis perennis* or lobelias. Set off the rich colours of ranunculus beautifully with tall, blue delphiniums as companions. Dorotheanthus makes a vivid carpet or edging for taller bulbs and annuals.

Treated tulips should only be planted in May in a place where they do no receive the hot afternoon sun. Make sure that any bulbs you buy are plump and healthy, with no sign of new leaves.

ROSES

Roses are especially richly coloured in autumn. Keep them company with bags of annuals in bloom. In years gone by the rule was to reduce their food and water in autumn, but current advice is to maintain feeding and watering to keep up leaf production until it's time for pruning.

CAMELLIAS AND AZALEAS

Camellia sasanqua, with its small, dark-green leaves and abundant attractive flowers, plays a lovely role in autumn. Cheat a little by buying the plants in bloom and planting them in the garden and into pots. Keep camellias well mulched (they love pine needles) and watered and they will not drop their buds.

Kurume azaleas are the first to bloom and are known for their pretty autumn leaves. They like the sun, but their roots must not be allowed to burn which means a good thick layer of mulch after deep watering. They must have acid soil.

AUTUMN FOLIAGE AND SEEDS

Savour the crisp air as you take long walks in your neighbourhood, searching out those trees which offer glorious autumn foliage and consider buying one or two for your garden. While the large trees are the most spectacular, there are smaller trees, shrubs and climbers which provide an annual harvest of sunset colours (see page 153).

No leaf should ever be destroyed. Even sweeping them up is not really necessary. They belong there, under the tree, to give back some of nature's goodness. If they do have to be removed, put them into bags with a little moisture, or place them on the compost heap.

Leaves take longer to break down than other plant material, and it is usually better to keep them separate. They also make good mulch.

Oxalis, seems to be at its best at this time of the year. It doesn't like lime, which can be dribbled into the centre of the plants, then watered in.

Collect dry flower seeds on a hot, dry autumn day; dust them with fungicide and store them in paper bags or bottles.

PLANTING EVERGREEN TREES

As we wonder at the beauty of deciduous trees in autumn splendour, it is well to look at the evergreen trees which bring shelter against wind and cold, and consider bringing one or two into the garden. Out-of-ground large trees are planted in June, so order them now and prepare the holes.

AUTUMN PLANTING

With the worst heat of summer over, autumn is a special time in the garden. Enjoy being surrounded by rich autumn colours and bright and shining berries borne with grace on even young plants.

Bougainvilleas can be planted in autumn. Place the bag in the hole and make slits in the sides and base of the bag, to prevent the soil mix falling away from the stem and possibly leading to the death of the plant. Roses are also happy to be planted in March, so they can settle down before winter. Take cuttings of impatiens and *Begonia semperflorens*.

Plant new shrubs in March. The following will provide splashes of gold in winter: *Duranta erecta* 'Sheena's Gold', *Euonymus japonicus* 'Aureus', golden elder, *Elaeagnus pungens* 'Maculata', *Melaleuca bracteata* 'Johannesburg Gold', *Phormium cookianum* 'Yellow Wave' and conifers *Cupressus macrocarpa* 'Donard Gold' and 'Goldcrest', *Platycladus orientalis* 'Golden Rocket' and *Cupressus sempervirens* 'Swane's Gold'.

Plant a calamondin (dwarf citrus) in a large container filled with rich, well-drained soil and placed in a sunny position. Keep it watered and it will bear a harvest of small golden fruit in winter.

In frosty areas protect tender and newly planted shrubs with a light-as-air protective fabric which floats over plants.

BELOW *Before it takes on its full autumn glory, this Japanese maple,* Acer palmatum, *goes through a lovely, mellow stage, looking rather like a well-worn, well-loved tapestry.*

PLANTING FOR WINTER AND SPRING

ANNUALS

Alcea rosea (hollyhock)
Antirrhinum majus (snapdragon)
Aquilegia caerulea (flowering columbine)
Bellis perennis (English daisy)
Calendula officinalis (English marigold)
Centaurea cyanus (cornflower)
Cheiranthus cheiri (wallflower)
Consolida ambigua (larkspur)
Delphinium x elatum (delphinium)
Dianthus spp.
Digitalis purpurea (foxglove)
Dorotheanthus bellidiformis (Bokbaai vygie)
Eschscholzia californica (Californian poppy)
Iberis umbellata (candytuft)
Lathyrus odoratus (sweet pea)
Linaria maroccana (toad flax)
Lobelia erinus
Lobularia maritima (alyssum)
Malcolmia maritima (Virginia stock)

Mimulus luteus (monkey flower)
Myosotis alpestris (forget-me-not)
Nemesia strumosa (Cape jewels)
Papaver spp. (poppy)
Petunia hybrids
Primula malacoides (fairy primrose)
Reseda odorata (mignonette)
Schizanthus pinnatus (butterfly flower)
Senecio hybrids (florist's cineraria)
Viola cornuta
Viola x wittrockiana (pansy)
Viscaria

PERENNIALS

Diascia integerrima (twinspur)
Gazania spp.
Heuchera sanguinea (coral bells)
Nierembergia repens (cup flower)
Penstemon hybrids
Scabiosa spp. (scabious)

Winter

The Western Cape is cold and wet, the sub-tropical areas are warm and dry and the inland plateau is very cold and dry. Trees, bare of leaves, display their majestic structure of trunk and branches against the winter sky. Aloes hold their flaming torches aloft, while their nectar brings the birds flocking. Mesembryanthemums cover the ground with their sparkling jewel-like colours. It is winter.

Frost may be about, coming on clear, windless nights. Take care when walking on a frosty lawn, as it could be dreadfully slippery. In frost-prone areas hoses should not be left with any water in them overnight, as they will crack.

HANDLING FROST

It may seem to be utterly destructive, but frost actually does perform the valuable function of breaking up the soil and killing off a number of insect pests. It does have its own beauty too, as its sparkling crystals settle on plants and structures. If seedlings are frosted over in the early morning, go out quickly and wash them down with the hose before the sun reaches them and burns the leaves. When the soil is frozen, its existing water content is then not available to the plants, so you should water well. An extremely light anti-frost covering is available from garden centres. This fabric virtually floats over plants, protecting them from frost. You may find that the lower end of the garden is more prone to frost.

MAGNIFICENT MAGNOLIAS

A magnolia tree in full flower at the end of winter is an uplifting sight, with its elegant flowers borne on bare branches, looking for all the world like settling birds. Magnolias need shelter from strong winds and they have fleshy roots which do not like to be disturbed. If you are apprehensive about introducing a spreading magnolia, there are the slender 'Pinkie', 'Susan' and 'Ricki' varieties.

BELOW *Each leaf, as it catches the first light of day, is etched in frost, each of its hairs trapping an infinitesimal icy crystal. For a short time it is a miracle of beauty. Then with the sun's warmth, it is gone.*

CAMELLIA CARE

Surely the loveliest among the winter-blooming shrubs must be the *Camellia japonica* and *C. reticulata* with their utterly gorgeous flowers and gleaming foliage. The japonicas have been with us for a long time, but the reticulatas were found in a secret valley in China early in the 20th century and introduced to a highly appreciative gardening world. They can take more sun that the others and bear large ornate flowers from winter into early spring.

Camellias need well-drained, acid soil but are not as particular about this as azaleas. Choose from the many enchanting shades of camellia on sale in your garden centre and treat your winter garden to one or more of these lovely shrubs. The foliage will come into new growth as soon as flowering is over. At this time apply a general fertilizer (not high in nitrogen and not near the main stem), water it in well and spread over a good acid mulch. Camellias make excellent container subjects. Plant them in a well-drained mixture of compost and soil and include a water retainer such as Terrasorb.

AZALEAS

August, the last month of winter, can be dreadfully windy and unpredictable. But this is the time when the azaleas start their pageant of bright colour, bringing the first signs of the new season.

The kurumes are the first to flower, then come the glorious colours of the indicas, and last of all the deciduous azaleas often grouped together as 'Mollis' azaleas. They all need an acid soil and good drainage. If there is doubt about the soil, incorporate an acid compost during planting. Keep this at a good level at all times, slightly dug in. Aluminium sulphate, lightly sprinkled around the plant and watered in, will also retain the acid level, as will a mulch of pine needles. If your soil is highly alkaline, grow azaleas in containers where you can control the soil.

Azaleas do not like the soil around them to be cultivated, as their feeding roots are just underneath the surface.

BULBS AND BULBOUS PLANTS

Keep bulbs well watered, but not water-logged. In June lilium bulbs can still be planted. Make sure you mark the spot.

You can also still divide existing clumps, dusting the bulbs with fungicide and replanting.

LEFT The Euphorbia pulcherrima *'Plenissima' (Ecke's flaming sphere or ram's horn poinsettia) is a spectacular form of the poinsettia which sets warm gardens alight with its crimson 'flowers' in winter. It needs a place in the sun, and should not be over-watered. If 'flowering' stems are to be cut for the vase, strip off any leaves the night before, cut the stems the following morning and place the lower few centimetres in boiling water for 10 seconds, then plunge into cold water. They will last much longer in the vase given this treatment.*

TREES AND SHRUBS FOR SPRING

Aloe spp.	*Kolkwitzia amabilis* (beauty bush)
Azalea hybrids	*Lavandula spp.* (lavender)
Bolusanthus speciosus (tree wisteria)	*Leucospermum spp.* (pincushion)
Brunfelsia pauciflora (yesterday, today and tomorrow)	*Ochna atropurpurea* (carnival bush)
Petrea volubilis (purple wreath)
Buddleja salviifolia (sage-leafed buddleja)	*Philadelphus coronarius* (mock orange)
Callistemon spp. (bottlebrush)	*Protea spp.*
Camellia spp.	*Prunus spp.* (flowering plum, cherry)
Chaenomeles speciosa (flowering quince)	*Rhododendron spp.* (azaleas)
Cornus florida 'Rubra' (pink dogwood)	*Rothmannia globosa* (September bells)
Dombeya rotundifolia (wild pear)	*Streptosolen jamesonii* (marmalade bush)
Erica spp.	*Tabebuia chrysotricha* (yellow trumpet tree)
Forsythia x intermedia 'Spectabilis'	*Viburnum spp.* (snowball bush)
Greyia sutherlandii (Natal bottlebrush)	*Virgilia oroboides* (keurboom)
Jasminum polyanthum (Chinese jasmine)	*Weigela florida*
Kerria japonica (Japanese rose)	*Wisteria sinensis* (Chinese wisteria)

PERENNIALS

Look out for rust on pelargoniums, especially in winter-rainfall areas. In August divide perennials and take cuttings of dahlias' new growth. You can also divide perennial primulas straight after flowering.

Divide water-lilies while dormant. Hellebores in bloom will be on sale. They like semi-shade and rich, well-drained soil.

Buy a selection of zonal pelargoniums (geraniums) for pots and hanging baskets, and, for instant colour on the patio, buy a few arctotis 'Flame' which have vivid orange flowers and silver leaves.

PLANTING TREES

June is the month when large, deciduous, out-of-ground trees, such as fruit trees and blossom trees, can be planted. Make square holes twice the size of the existing root system and mix good garden soil with compost or other organic matter and superphosphate (see page 34).

PRUNING

July is the month to prune fruit trees, so get those pruning tools sharpened. Hydrangeas can also be pruned now. Cut any weak or dead stems down completely, then cut back other stems to where there are two fat and healthy buds. If you really do want huge flower heads, all the stems can be cut down, but flowering will be greatly delayed. In all the temperate climatic regions, roses should be pruned from the middle towards the end of July. Delay this task until August in cold regions.

Orange trees are bearing their golden fruit which stays on the tree for some time and need not be picked all at once. Prune the trees after fruiting. Then dig a shallow trench within the drip line, fill it with compost mixed with 2:3:2 and water well.

Carry out maintenance on trellises and pergolas when creepers and climbers have been cut back. *See pages 159 – 162 for more information on pruning.*

CONTAINER PLANTS

Some of these may have to be brought under shelter for the cold months, as the plants and even the containers themselves may be damaged by frost. Terracotta pots with a seam down the side, indicating their factory origin, are more prone to splitting than others. Make sure that you have some pots and plants tough enough to stay out on a sheltered, sunny patio, as you'll be spending much time there

BELOW *Flowering in late winter, the common coral tree* (Erythrina lysistemon) *towers over the wisteria whose fragrant clusters of purple and lilac flowers adorn its bare branches from late winter into spring.*

SPECIAL CARE

Proteas and other plants whose natural habitat is the Western Cape will find the dry winters in other parts hard to bear and will need regular watering. Bulbs and annuals will be coming on now and will need regular feeding with liquid manure or a general fertilizer, plus watering. As water is retained for longer in winter's cold soil, be careful not to over-water.

Birds will be in need of special care during the icy months. They will certainly need water and food. If you do start feeding them, it would be unfair not to keep up the routine. Give them a variety, like fruit, bonemeal (which they love), seed and even peanut-butter sandwiches.

Towards the end of winter, top-dress the lawn or apply a slow-release fertilizer.

in winter. Surround yourself with bright flowers, hang planted baskets from the pergola, then settle down with your magazines and gardening books and plan for the next season.

Cyclamens are a lovely part of winter. Keep them in a draught-free room where the air is cool and not over-heated. Water around the corm, not over the plant, keeping the soil damp but not water-logged. Feed them with Nitrosol every week or 10 days.

PLANTING FOR SPRING

Winter is the time to prepare for the glory of spring. It may seem that the cold, short days will never come to an end, but the buds made last summer are just waiting for the warmth that will bring them to life again.

Soon it will be time for primulas and poppies, pansies and petunias, and fruit trees covered in the trembling, innocent new blossoms of spring.

Violas, freesias, daffodils, anemones and a multitude of flowers will bring forth the first notes of colour until gradually growing into the veritable explosion which is the end of winter, the beginning of spring.

As winter draws to a close, plant annual seedlings in rich soil and feed and water regularly.

GARDENING TOOLS

Every gardener needs a basic range of tools. Gradually add to your selection as you discover tasks you are likely to repeat often. Buy the best quality you can afford and look after them – cleaning, drying and storing them in a dry indoor area.

Most garden centres have sharpening facilities for spades or cutting tools, so keep yours in good condition.

Have power tools regularly serviced for safety and efficiency. Keep a bucket of soil soaked in oil in the garden shed for this purpose. After use, place your garden tools in this.

DIGGING AND RAKING

If these tools are drably coloured, it will pay you handsomely to paint them a bright red or orange, so they will show up easily and save you many hours searching for that elusive small trowel or fork.

- A pick to break up clay or heavy soil when making beds.
- A good sturdy spade and a garden fork. There are smaller ones, easier for women and people of small build to use.
- A sturdy trowel and hand-fork.
- A wire rake for breaking up clods of soil and levelling beds, and a plastic- or rubber-pronged rake for gathering up leaves and grass.
- A weeding tool with a narrow blade.

WATERING

- A watering can with a long spout and detachable rose.
- A hose or hoses. They come in varying lengths, with durability guarantees indicated in time-spans, and some are already fitted for attaching to the tap.
- Explore the wide range of attachments, including sophisticated sprinklers and extenders to water hanging-baskets above head-height, now available to snap on to a universal hose-end.
- You may want to invest in an irrigation system with or without an automatic timer system.

GENERAL

- A wheelbarrow. Galvanized metal will last longer. A wheelbarrow with a rubber tyre is bliss to use.
- Garden gloves are essential. Fabric and suede are supple, and superb extended rubber-and-fabric gloves which are resistant to rose thorns are now available.
- A spirit level, a long tape measure and roll of strong string for the laying out of beds or if you want to make new levels in your garden.
- A smooth wooden plank – with two holes drilled at each end, a rope handle threaded through each pair and a cushion on top – makes a good 'kneeler' when weeding or planting.

FOR YOUR LAWN

- A power lawn mower. Most mowers these days are the rotary kind and those operated by electricity, rather than petrol, are becoming more widespread.
- A nylon-line trimmer and safety goggles to protect your eyes. Always use the safety goggles.

PRUNING

- Clippers, loppers and secateurs.
- Hedge shears or a hedge trimmer. If you buy a power model, check that it has a guarantee and that spare parts are readily available.
- A pruning saw and a bow saw.

Maintenance

To keep your garden at its best, some tasks must be repeated year after year, season after season. Looking after the soil and the health of your plants, watering well and regularly, watching the progress of your plants carefully, combatting pests and diseases – these are all essential for your little piece of paradise to flourish.

Waterwise gardening

The wise use of precious water, so scarce in our country, means either choosing plants which need the barest minimum of water, or applying water wisely and effectively.

WATER RETAINERS

Water retainers such as Terrasorb are jelly-like substances which can expand greatly and absorb water, which is then taken up by plants as they need it. It is certainly not possible to use a water retainer freely throughout the garden because of its cost. However, as it can last for several years and can save up to 50 per cent of water, it is worth using for those special plants. In fact, many gardeners, when buying a rose or a new shrub, add the water retainer to the cost, as they do with compost and food.

WATERING BY HAND-HELD HOSE

There are various spray heads for watering by hand-held hose, including attachments for delivering fertilizer through the hose while you water. Watering by hose enables you to direct the water just where it is needed, plus have a close look at each plant, to smell the hot earth as it takes in the water, to see a chameleon stretching out to a wet leaf, or a family of happy birds flying through an arch of spray.

Different attachments serve different purposes. Try to use an attachment that is tailor-made for the task at hand in terms of reach, output and distribution. An overhead sprinkler's reach must be higher than the highest plant. Take care when watering plants with long arching strap leaves: the water will run partly down to the centre, but partly down to the tips of the leaves beyond the root run. One drawback of overhead sprinklers is that they water each and every plant within their radius regardless of its water needs. Another drawback is that on a windy day too fine a mist may just blow away.

IRRIGATION SYSTEMS

Look into all that is available when you are considering a watering system, weighing up the varying needs of plants. There are underground and above-ground systems which will surely save much time, but expert opinion is virtually essential. Water pressure must be sufficient; sprinkler heads must be correctly selected and placed; and a plan must be made for the system to be divided up into various circuits

---

WATERING LAWNS

How often a lawn needs to be watered, depends on the following factors:

- soil – clay absorbs water slowly and must be watered slowly (spike it to keep it aerated); sandy soil must be watered more often;
- the micro-climate – hot spells demand more water, wind dries the grass and makes spraying difficult, shady areas need less water unless competing tree roots are present;
- slope – here you should water more often, but for shorter periods and keep the lawn aerated and free of thatch;
- variety of grass – some varieties are more tolerant of dry conditions; some deeper-rooted grasses need deeper watering, but less often (*see* page 55).

so that lawns, beds and shrubs can each be watered in their own way and only when they need it. Irrigation systems can include:

- Surface or buried pipes with a selection of spray-heads: standard, variable arcs or pop-up, with control valves where and if necessary.
- Drip water heads which provide each plant with its own water supply by means of regular drips.
- A control system or timer to turn the water on and off at specified times. (A manually operated system does not need control valves or a control system.)

If you lay polythene water pipes through the garden, either bury them at a good depth down in the soil, or are lay them on the surface. It is so easy to dig down a spade's depth, then hear an ominous swish of water gushing through a sliced pipe.

GROW THE RIGHT PLANTS

Choose plants which are adapted to your local rainfall patterns. Shrubs are often planted in autumn in the summer-rainfall areas so that they can settle down and deal with heavy summer rain.

Advice from your garden centre, the Botanical Society and neighbouring gardeners will lead you to plants from other areas which will also do well. You will be amazed to discover what you can grow with the barest minimum of water. You will also find that nearly all indigenous plants need a well-drained soil.

GROUP FOR WATERING

Your basic aim is to water only those plants which need it. Plan your garden, placing plants needing regular watering near the house and those with lesser needs further away. This method saves time if you water by hand and enables you to plan your irrigation system accordingly if you use one.

However you water, newly planted seedlings (in fact any newly planted plants) are the first priority. In a mixed border of roses, watsonias, day lilies, small shrubs and annuals, the roses and seedlings must receive their quota of water, while the others can wait till next time.

REDUCE YOUR LAWN AREA

A lawn needs a great deal of water to keep it looking good. You certainly will save water if you replace at least part of your lawn with paving, a waterwise groundcover, a waterwise flower bed or shrubbery.

Choose a low-maintenance, waterwise grass, preferably indigenous to your climatic region. To ensure that the water gets down to the roots, aerate the lawn by spiking it with a garden fork.

CULTIVATE THE SOIL

Compost helps the soil retain moisture, it promotes earthworm activity and, as it breaks down, it adds nutrients, strengthening the plant and enabling it to withstand water shortages and disease.

Water retainers (crystals or gel) do what they say. When you mix them into the soil they swell to two or three hundred times their volume and retain water for the plants to absorb as they need it. This will save a lot of water in containers which hold roses or other precious plants.

Check the soil before you water. On a hot day the surface may look dry, but if you push your finger down into the soil, you will probably find it is quite damp a few centimetres down.

BELOW Nerine bowdenii, *also known as the Guernsey lily, is one of our spectacular indigenous summer-flowering bulbs. They do well in the shade or semi-shade in hot, dry areas, but must be watered well throughout the growing season.*

WATERING GUIDELINES

- Deep watering is necessary, as light sprinkling will bring roots up near to the surface where they may be baked by the sun. A shallow-rooted plant may also be more unstable and liable to be uprooted in strong wind.
- Basins around shrubs will ensure that the water sinks down where it is needed.
- Mulching is vital as it prevents evaporation of the precious water and keeps roots cool.
- Well-fed plants use what water they get more efficiently than under-nourished ones.
- It is always better to water the garden so there is time for the plants to dry off before night-fall, to avoid fungal diseases. The cool of the morning is a good time for watering.
- Certain plants such as hydrangeas and fuchsias may look sad and wilted in the midday sun, but if you are sure you have given them enough water, leave them and they will revive in the cool of the evening.
- Don't water at midday when it is very hot and wasteful evaporation will be high.

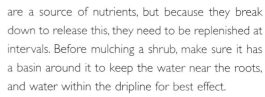

BELOW Clivia miniata, the flame of the forest, has gained fame locally and overseas where many hybrids have been brought to a large following of this magnificent indigenous plant. Different shapes and colours are much sought after. Clivias grow well in containers. In the garden they will need shade, a loose friable soil and water in dry spells and dry regions.

Weeds take up precious water and should be destroyed as soon as they show their leaves above the soil. Either hoe them out gently, try cutting them to the ground with a pair of sharp scissors, or make a shallow trench between perennials and shrubs, place the weeds in the trench (make sure there are not flowers on them) and cover with soil.

LAY DOWN MULCH

Mulch can consist of compost, pine needles, pine bark, groundnut shells, hay, sawdust or wood chips (add nitrogen). You can even lay down old underfelt after you have watered thoroughly. Pebbles, too, can be decorative as well as effective. Organic mulches

are a source of nutrients, but because they break down to release this, they need to be replenished at intervals. Before mulching a shrub, make sure it has a basin around it to keep the water near the roots, and water within the dripline for best effect.

The advantages of mulch are:
- It keeps weeds at bay.
- It retains moisture by preventing evaporation.
- It prevents washaway erosion.
- It keeps the soil warm in winter and cool in summer.
- It is the basis of good topsoil.

MAXIMIZE AVAILABLE WATER

Roof tanks for rainfall collection are becoming more and more evident on private properties. It is amazing how much water you can collect off the roof (a litre per square metre for every millimetre of rainfall). But before you buy a tank, make sure that there are no municipal regulations forbidding this because of the danger of mosquitoes breeding. Even if it is permitted, a permanent film of paraffin or cooking oil should kept be on the water's surface.

Install one of the commercially available systems to redirect bath and shower water into the garden.

To take water down to the roots of shrubs and small trees where it is needed, hammer pipes into the ground, or take off the bottom of a plastic cool drink bottle and place this, neck down, into the soil, leaving just a few centimetres above soil level. Keep the pipes or bottles filled with water. Place containers on drip trays or saucers so that the water will flow through into them, to be taken up once more and not wasted.

The merciless sun will take up precious water from the soil, but even the slightest shade will cut this down enormously, so give some thought to a few more shade trees.

Knowing the water needs of your plants will enable you to work out an effective programme of water saving, and you will come to know, more than ever, the immense value of this precious substance which is the basis of life and without which we would surely perish.

Pruning

A rose plant or a plum tree left to its own devices will grow into a tangle of intertwining stems, many of which will die away, or become woody and unproductive. Judicious pruning will result in a healthy plant and a good crop of flowers or fruit.

WHY PRUNE?

Basically, pruning aims to take out any unwanted growth in order to improve the shape of a plant, then to cut back existing growth in order to stimulate new, vigorous growth (while the plant receives a healthy diet).

WHAT YOU NEED

For pruning you will need a pair of very sharp secateurs, and for those very thick stems, or for long thorny stems, a pair of loppers. A pruning saw is useful for tackling branches thicker than about 2,5 cm. For thorny subjects such as roses and berry fruit, you will need a stout pair of gloves with long sleeves.

ROSES

With good care, roses will produce a large number of healthy stems and leaves which last from spring to winter. However when the cold winter comes, it is time to virtually create a new plant. In the next growing season this plant must give rise to a whole new generation of leaves and stems, and then a wealth of beautiful blooms.

In warm, frost-free areas pruning can start as early as the first week of July, while in colder parts it can be delayed until the end of July or into August. There must be no more danger of frost, which could kill off any new tender growth.

Although each rose grower has his own special time for and approach to pruning, a completely new method has been introduced (see page 160).

Hybrid tea roses and floribundas

A week before pruning spray the bush with lime sulphur, one in eight parts of water. Start pruning by taking out any dead, diseased or straggling stems. The first thing to do is to cut the entire bush down to about 75 cm in height. You will now be left with a group of stems rising from the ground, some fresh green, some with a greyish look. Choose three or four of the green stems. If there are not enough, you can retain an older one. Cut all the others right off, down to the ground. Then make sure the tops of the remaining ones are quite level and take off any lingering leaves. Give the bush another dose of lime sulphur. Roses with weak growth should be cut back more severely than those in abundantly good health.

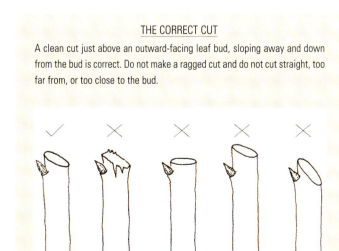

THE CORRECT CUT

A clean cut just above an outward-facing leaf bud, sloping away and down from the bud is correct. Do not make a ragged cut and do not cut straight, too far from, or too close to the bud.

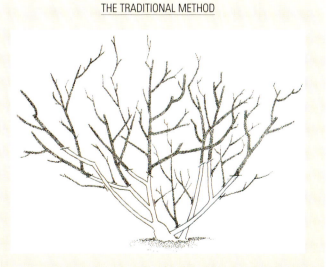

THE TRADITIONAL METHOD

Miniature roses

These should be cut down to about 10 cm in height, with any old or dead stems taken off down to the ground. Cut thin side stems to about 20 cm, or leave them alone if this is to time-consuming.

English roses (David Austin roses)

These grow tall, with slender arching stems, and should not be cut back too severely. Rather take out any weak stems right down to the ground, then trim any extra-long stems.

Climbers, ramblers and heritage roses

Some climbers may have grown beyond your reach, up trees and high walls. Those which can be reached can have their flowered stems cut away completely, leaving new long stems to be tied down along the fence or other support. These can then be cut back from the tip if necessary, and their side stems shortened to about 15 cm. A pretty idea is to bend some of the stems over into an arc, which will encourage their side stems to flower profusely. The timing of pruning is different for ramblers, which should be cut back immediately after flowering.

Some of the old climbing forms of hybrid teas such as 'Peace' and 'Crimson Glory' should not have

PRUNING A CLIMBING ROSE

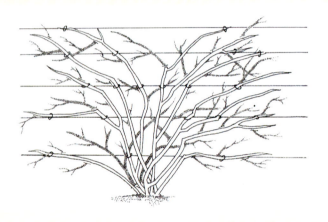

THE NEW METHOD OF ROSE PRUNING

The traditional method is the normal practice for many gardeners. Now a cat has been set among the rose pigeons by renowned grower Ludwig Taschner who lives with – and loves – roses. He advises a new method of pruning which he says provides more foliage, and thus more flowers.

The new method means cutting the plants cleanly to knee height and leaving existing stems and side shoots intact. "My approach to rose growing is leaves, leaves, leaves," says Ludwig, "With this new approach to pruning we simply start that much earlier in the season to stimulate root growth through leaf activity ... the side shoots and twiggy growth ... will sprout more quickly in the new season ... encouraging root activity long before the leaves from the main stems can do so ... Once the new upper shoots are really growing ... they take over the function of the twiggy shoots which by then are shaded from the sunlight and will soon shrivel and die ... Previously ... we were certainly not aware enough of the importance of early green leaves feeding the roots ..."

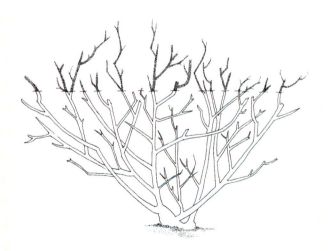

their long canes reduced, but rather tied horizontally. Once modern climbers such as 'Compassion', 'High hopes', 'Isidingo' and 'Blossom Magic' have filled their allotted space, any loose hanging canes or those which have grown too high can be cut away.

Heritage roses which bloom in spring, including banksias and eglantynes, are cut back after flowering. 'Albertine' with its vigorous growth, is cut back at the end of November.

Feeding

During winter pruning when roots are dormant, the soil around the plants can be disturbed. Dig in copious amounts of compost, manure, superphosphate and bonemeal, taking care not to touch the main stem or loosen strong roots.

Summer pruning

Take out dead and weak growth of bush roses and cut stems back by a third. This will give a crop of gorgeous, richly coloured autumn roses, ready for autumn flower shows. Forty to 45 days will elapse between pruning and blooming.

TREES

To shape trees, prune them when they are young (deciduous trees in winter, evergreen trees in spring). Remove criss-crossed light inner branches and dead and weak growth and prune the tree lightly to the correct shape. To stop a tree at a required height, cut out the leading branch at that height.

If you have a large, precious tree that needs attention as a result of storm damage or if you suspect it may be diseased and need saving, it will be worth engaging the services of a reputable tree expert.

Fruit trees

The aim of pruning is to establish three or four main branches which are spaced around the main stem about 20 cm apart, the lowest about 40 cm from ground level. Cut the main stem to about 75 cm, then cut back any side stems to the same length. New growth will arise from the main stem and these side stems. The following year these should be cut back by about two-thirds and they will each in turn give rise to two or three new side stems. At the right time these will be cut back and in the third year you should have a well-shaped tree, with about twelve healthy stems around the main trunk.

After this, pruning should be less harsh and the normal principles of pruning should be followed. Prune hard for weak growth and prune lightly for vigorous growth.

REMOVING A LARGE BRANCH FROM A TREE

Remove smaller side branches.

Remove branch with a rough cut from above and below.

Make the last cut just outside the branch collar. Do not cut into the bark ridge.

MAKING A STANDARD SHRUB (SUCH AS A FUCHSIA)

Strike a nice, straight cutting in a pot, positioning a stake close to it for future support. As the cutting grows, continue to support it by tying it to the stake. Gently rub off any side stems, but keep the top leaves. Once the stem has reached the required height (from 60 to 150 cm) pinch out the central growth to prevent the stem from growing upwards, and to encourage side growth. When side stems form, pinch back their terminal buds two or three times to ensure a bushy shape before allowing the flowers to develop.

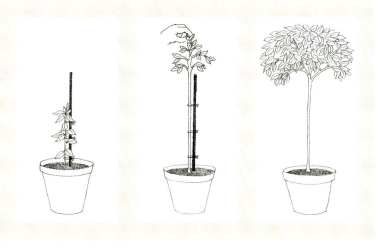

FLOWERING SHRUBS

These should, on the whole, be pruned after flowering. Spring bloomers such as azaleas should be cut only if a better shape is needed. Spiraeas can be cut back hard when flowering is over. Weigelas can form a great deal of wood and all woody stems should be cut back to the ground.

Hydrangeas can be pruned in autumn by taking out old wood with rough bark, as well as dead wood, right down to the ground. Flowered stems can be cut back to where there are two fat buds.

Hibiscus are best pruned by cutting out tangled or weak stems right at ground level.

Fuchsias are cut back to a number of healthy stems, then the terminal growth pinched back several times to encourage bushy growth.

HEDGES

Whatever kind of hedge you choose it will need some trimming. Always clip a hedge so that it is wider at the bottom than at the top. In this way the upper leaves do not shade the lower ones, and the hedge is more stable in strong winds.

Some hedging plants are allowed to grow at will, to create a loosely growing informal hedge and this will probably only need an annual trim to keep it looking attractive.

A formal hedge needs regular clipping to be kept in good shape. To create a formal hedge, start pruning when the young plants have sent out side shoots, which should be cut back to about half their length twice or three times during their first season. Trim the main shoots to keep all plants to an even height.

A neglected old hedge can be renovated if you proceed with care. Be careful with conifers, though, as most will not respond with new growth if ther are cut back hard.

For other hedges, tackle the job over two years or two pruning seasons. During the first pruning season, trim one side normally, but cut the other side right back to get the plants to send out healthy new growth. Fertilize and water the hedge to help it along. The next year, clip the new growth lightly, but cut the other side of the hedge right back.

A hedge is clipped to be wider at the bottom than at the top.

A formal hedge requires regular clipping.

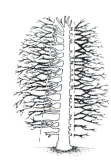

An old hedge is renovated in two stages.

CLIMBERS

Various climbers are pruned in various ways, depending on whether they flower on current or older wood, or how vigorous their growth is. Generally they are only pruned to restrict their size, and only when they become almost overgrown. Be especially careful that a climber does not get out of control near guttering, roof tiles or the like.

A general rule for timing is to prune non-flowering climbers just before spring, and flowering climbers some time after flowering.

In winter cut back all side shoots of wisteria and grape vines to within 10 cm of the old wood and remove any spindly, long stems completely. Clematis montana does not like to be cut back, but the hybrids can be cut back hard in autumn.

PRUNING A CLIMBER

Reduce the side growth and remove old or woody main stems to make room for new growth.

Trim self-clinging plants *in situ*. Other climbers may have to be removed from their support before pruning.

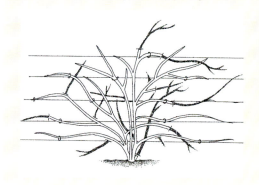

PRUNING TIPS

- In days of drought don't be tempted to cut shrubs back in the belief that they will have less growth to contend with. Cutting back will make them feel they have to produce more growth, which means more water.
- Standard roses and many other standard shrubs are grafted on to stock of different varieties, so if the tall stem breaks, the top growth will be destroyed, and the stock will not give rise to more of the same plant.

Propagation

A few generations back, virtually the only way of obtaining new plants was to take cuttings or seeds from one's own or from friends' gardens. Now we have splendid garden centres to provide us with a wonderful selection of healthy plants. Nevertheless we all have an urge to try our hand at propagating plants, for economy or the delight of having multiple offspring from a very special plant.

Two main ways of propagation are vegetative (or asexual) and sexual. Vegetative propagation is by means of cuttings, new bulbs, runners, stolons, corms, leaf cuttings, budding, grafting, dividing or layering. All of these involve part of the plant itself, and result in plants identical to the original. Most important of all, they cost nothing.

Sexual propagation means the coming together of pollen (male) and ovary (female), sometimes on the same flower, sometimes on different flowers, even different plants, but always on flowers of the same species. The result is a seed. Seeds cannot be relied upon to produce plants identical to the parents, and this is how all the hybrids or crosses arise.

VEGETATIVE PROPAGATION

You will need a place sheltered from wind and sun, a sharp knife, secateurs, containers, soil, plastic cool drink bottles or plastic bags to serve as miniature greenhouses, and labels. A mist spray and a pot of hormone powder will help enormously but are not essential. Hormone powder is available in three variants, for softwood, semi-hardwood and hardwood cuttings. Cuttings should be taken from healthy young plants, never from diseased plants.

Softwood cuttings

Softwood cuttings are taken in spring and early summer, from new growth. Take a cutting of 10 – 15 cm, making a clean cut just below a joint or node. Take off the lower leaves. If the leaves are very large, cut the top few leaves in half. Dip the lower end of softwood cuttings in hormone powder and plant them as soon as possible into clean coarse sand which, although it has no nutrients, is disease-free and aerated. When the cuttings are well rooted they can be transferred to a good potting mixture, either bought from your garden centre or made yourself.

A good mix is two parts sieved leafmould, three parts sand, and a sprinkling of vermiculite to help to keep the soil open.

Plastic cool drink bottles form marvellous miniature greenhouses. Merely cut off and discard the clear plastic base. Place what is left of the bottle over the cuttings after they have been watered. A container of cuttings can also be placed into a plastic bag greenhouse.

Semi-hardwood cuttings

These are taken from firm, new shoots of evergreens such as camellias during early to late summer, with that current season's growth yielding the cuttings. They should be about 10 – 15 cm in length, cut just below a node.

Hardwood cuttings

Hardwood cuttings are taken from autumn to early spring. Take them from ripe wood grown the previous year. They must be without leaves, 18 – 20 cm long and have at least two nodes. Strike them in a trench or in sizeable pots and keep them watered.

BELOW *At the height of summer, agapanthus are a profusion of blue, with charmingly rounded heads of pink dahlias to compete with them. Dahlias can be propagated by tuber division or cuttings in summer. They prefer a sunny position and the plants should never be allowed to dry out.*

Leaf cuttings

African violet leaves are removed, together with a portion of stem, and the stem is inserted into sand and peat moss. When new plants form, they should be gently removed and planted into individual pots.

Begonias, streptocarpus and gloxinias can have the veins on their underside cut through, then the leaf laid underside down on damp sand and weighted down. Their leaves can also be cut into portions and half submerged in the sand. A healthy leaf from a sansevieria can also be cut into sections and these planted upright in sand.

Runners

Runners are stems which arise in a leaf axil, and extend to make new plants away from the parent plant. The new plants can be cleanly separated and planted out in other locations. The strawberry is the best-known plant to propagate this way.

BELOW RIGHT The indigenous arum lily, Zantedeschia pentlandii, likes to get its feet well down into the soil. It is propagated by means of root division.

PROPAGATION TIPS

- When a cordyline becomes leggy, cut the stem right back to about half a metre above the ground, cut the removed stem into 20 cm lengths, plant upright and keep them damp.
- Choose a mature stem of a dieffenbachia, remove the upper, leafy part, cut the remainder into 10 cm pieces and lay them horizontally on damp sand.
- Citrus peel, which contains growth hormones, should never be thrown away. Soak it in water which can then be used on seedlings and cuttings.

Stolons

Stolons are stems which, when in contact with the soil, form new plantlets.

Suckers

These come from underground to create new plants, which may in turn be separated.

Bulbs, corms, tubers and rhizomes

Bulbs and corms produce new small bulbs and corms. When the leaves have withered, lift the clump, clean it up, dry it and then divide it. Store the old and new bulbs and corms in a dry, cool spot and plant them out the following autumn.

Lilies can be propagated from the scales of their bulbs. Carefully detach the healthy outer scales and dust them with fungicide. Then either plant them to

BULBS, CORMS AND SCALES

Bulblets

Dividing corms

Detaching healthy outer scales

Planted in a clear plastic bag with compost

half their depth in a container of moist compost which you cover with a plastic bag, or place them in a clear plastic bag of moist compost, tied tightly and kept in a warm place. In about six weeks small bulblets will form at the base of the scales. Plant these out, directly into the soil or first in small pots.

Dahlias propagate themselves by means of tubers. During the growing season the plant produces new tubers underground. When you lift these, clumps of fat tubers are connected to the old, dead stem or stems. In separating a tuber from the clump, it is essential to also take part of the stem. You can also wait until new shoots are sent out from the clump, cut these cleanly away and plant them in pots until they are rooted and producing new growth.

Rhizomes (irises and cannas) can be cut into sections, each with a bud. Lift irises every four to five years and cut off plump, healthy new rhizomes on the outside of the clump. Cut their leaves down to half their size and replant them with the top of the rhizome above ground. The remaining leaves will shade the rhizome.

Divide cannas every two to three years or they will become very overcrowded and produce smaller flowers. Removing flowered stems regularly will ensure healthy growth of the remaining stems.

Layering
Layering means bending down (not detaching) a stem from the mother plant, and, after making a slit on its underside, burying this section in the soil and

DIVIDING RHIZOMES
When dividing rhizomes, ensure that each section has a bud. Cut leaves right back and plant each section with the top of the rhizome above ground level.

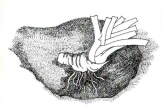

PROPAGATION BY LAYERING

Making a slit on underside of stem   *Burying stem in soil after pegging it down*

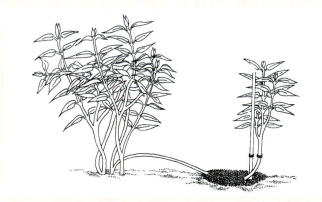

Formation of root system and leaves indicate that new plant can be detached

DIVIDING FINE- AND TUBEROUS-ROOTED PERENNIALS

Gently teasing fine-rooted perennials apart   *Dividing tuberous-rooted perennials*   *Using two forks to pry apart dense clumps*

weighing or pegging it down. When a good root system and leaves have formed, the new plant may be detached.

Division of perennials

Clumps of perennials can be divided in autumn or spring, taking the outer sturdy growth for transplanting. Fine-rooted perennials can be pulled apart by hand, but for the tougher rooted ones you will need a spade or two forks to pry them apart.

SEED (SEXUAL) PROPAGATION

When a pollen grain alights on a flower it grows into a tube, which then extends down into the ovary of the flower, to unite and form a seed. This is surely one of Nature's many miracles. Within the seed, whether it be minute or large, lie the makings of a new plant, perfectly protected. The seed can be transported to other areas with safety and there it can remain, sometimes for years, to be brought to life by water and warmth. A plant from a seed is not always identical to the parent, which makes growing from seed quite exciting.

Direct sowing

You can sow seeds on to the soil's surface, which should be level, free of weeds, enriched with organic material and finely tilled. Either plant the seeds in shallow trenches or scatter them lightly over the surface. Rake it over very lightly and cover it with a thin layer of sand. Mark the sown area with a few pegs and keep it well moistened.

When the new seedlings have two or more leaves they can be thinned out and the surplus either discarded, or planted out elsewhere. When they are growing well, give them a dose of watered-down liquid manure, the colour of weak tea, or a sprinkling of general fertilizer well watered in.

Sowing in seed trays

Use a commercial seedling mix, or one you have made from sand and peat-moss in equal quantities, with a sprinkling of vermiculite. Dampen the mix before planting, then take the greatest care sowing the seeds. Some seeds are very fine and can easily be sown too thickly. This will mean a great loss of plants as they grow in too-dense clumps. Cover the seeds with a sprinkling of fine sand, water them well and cover the trays with glass, which you must turn over each day. Some gardeners prefer to cover the trays with newspaper, which is removed once germination has taken place. A dusting of fungicide or Bordeaux mix on the seedlings will help prevent damping off (a fungal disease which causes seedlings to collapse). Once they have four leaves they can planted out into separate pots or compartmentalized punnets, then into the open ground.

BELOW Nemesias, one of our most popular indigenous anuals, have been hybridised into rich, glowing, jewel colours. Nemesia strumosa has provided the most colourful flowers. Sow seeds in autumn, or plant seedlings into well-drained soil in full sun or semi-shade. The violas keeping these nemesias company need the same conditions.

SEED TIPS
- Use a caster sugar shaker to sow tiny seeds evenly.
- After sowing seeds in a tray, place blotting paper over them. This will ensure that water is gently dispersed. The blotting paper will disintegrate before the seedlings are ready for transplanting.

Pests and diseases

We no longer live in a Garden of Eden and there are always some pests and plant diseases about. That is nature's way and we just have to keep these problems within bounds. But we should all have a sense of responsibility for our environment in every aspect of dealing with pests and diseases.

RULES FOR DEFENCE

There are two main rules for restricting attack by pests and diseases:

- Keep your plants in vigorous good health, because it is always the weaklings which are the first to be attacked.
- Ensure your garden is neat and tidy, so that there are no spots where the enemies can lurk, before they come in to attack.

CONSIDER NATURE

We tend our plants lovingly and take pleasure in watching their healthy growth. Then suddenly one morning a precious rose may be covered in beetles, the underside of nasturtium leaves may be black with aphids, or rose leaves may look sick and yellow, a sure sign of black spot. Deep despair follows, and we rush off to consult our books, or we take a specimen to the garden centre, where we will be told of all the treatments available. Research is constantly being carried out into the various pests which attack our plants. Great progress has been made in producing disease-resistant plants such as rust-resistant antirrhinums and various effective treatments have been found for various pests.

While farmers and other large-scale growers use chemicals thankfully, it might be well for gardeners to consider that chemicals may not only kill the problem insects, but a multitude of useful ones, creating a chain of destruction. When aphids are sprayed, they may be eaten by mantids, which are eaten by lizards or birds. The whole chain is badly affected.

FUNGI, BACTERIA AND VIRUSES

The main problems gardeners are forced to contend with are the fungi, bacteria and viruses; the insects, slugs and snails; and the weeds. For each of them there is a remedy.

Fungi attack plants by getting deep down into their tissue. They flourish when the sky is overcast and there is high humidity, and where plants grow so close together that they cannot dry off. Fungi are everywhere in the air, waiting to settle on a suitable host. If a plant is found to be completely taken over by a fungus, it is better to take it out and destroy it.

If one plant among others of the same species (roses for example) is affected, then all these plants must be sprayed. Make sure that every part of the plant, and the soil around it, is well covered with spray, so that any fungal spores alighting will immediately succumb.

Black spot

Probably the worst of the fungal diseases is the dreaded black spot on roses, which causes leaves to turn yellow with black spots, then brown, and eventually die and fall off. There are fungicides to deal with this, and since prevention is vastly better than cure, spraying should be started early in the season. All the affected leaves should be picked off and destroyed. A simple way of doing this as you work your way through the plant is to hold an old kitchen

---

PRECAUTIONS WHEN USING CHEMICALS

When you resort to chemicals which could cause illness and even worse, handle them with the greatest care. Here are some important precautions:

- Keep all your potentially dangerous chemicals in a cool, locked cupboard, or on a shelf well above child height.
- Labels should be kept legible. It's a good idea to protect the label with plastic and cellotape, and, as an extra precaution, to tie a descriptive label around the bottle neck.
- Out-of-date chemicals should be destroyed.
- Never store liquids in cooldrink bottles, which could be a possibly fatal temptation to curious or thirsty children.
- Always follow the instructions exactly and do not decide that twice as much will be twice as effective.
- During mixing and application, take care that chemicals do not come into contact with your skin. Wear all-enveloping clothing plus a disposable nose-and-mouth mask if necessary and wash all exposed areas immediately afterwards.
- Wait for the full period dictated between spraying edible crops and picking them. The chemical won't simply wash off the fruit or vegetable under the tap.

sieve under the leaves and collect them as they easily fall off. Then destroy these leaves completely. Never put diseased material on the compost heap.

Other common fungi

Rust is a pernicious fungus which is well named. Other fungi causing disease are powdery mildew (powdery white growth on leaves and tender new shoots, with possibly distorted leaves), downy mildew (white to greyish fluffy growth mostly under leaves) and botrytis (grey fluffy growth on fruit, flowers, leaves and stems). For these, fungicides are usually the answer.

Lawn fungi

Various fungi can attack the lawn, and should be dealt with as early as possible. If you see a change in colour, or notice a white deposit on the lawn, remove the affected grass and destroy it. Then spray the surrounding grass with a fungicide and bring in fresh soil and compost to the vacant area.

Three fungus diseases that may affect lawns are brown patch (dry, circular patches turning brown); dollar spot (vivid brown spots, about 5 cm across); rust and leafspot (purplish spots on blades). These may occur when the lawn is undernourished, the soil too compacted, too much high-nitrogen fertilizer has been used or the lawn has been watered at night. Remedy these factors and also spray the area with copper oxychloride or permanganate of potash, five times at intervals of 10 days.

Bacteria and viruses

Bacteria and viruses cause dreadful disfigurements, especially in vegetables and fruit. Leaves can be puckered and distorted, flowers distorted and discoloured. Completely destroy every single affected plant or part of plant and seek advice from experts.

INSECTS AND OTHER PESTS

Beetles, flies, worms and caterpillars all relish dining on your garden plants. Insecticides have been developed for dealing with them, including systemic insecticides which enter into a plant's tissues and are ingested by the insects.

Some insects, like CUTWORMS, lurk underground. Others chew stems, leaves and even flowers.

SPRAYING GUIDELINES

- Keep one sprayer solely for spraying garden chemicals. Always clean it out thoroughly after use. Don't leave the wetting agent in the sprayer, as this could clog its narrow pipes.
- Spray only on a calm day and at the time of day recommended in the instructions.
- Do not use weedkillers near water features or children's play areas.
- At the first sign of disease, or at the first sighting of aphids, beetles or other insects, don't delay. Spray them at once, or preferably pick them off.
- A wetting agent (Teepol or Sunlight liquid) will help the liquid to stick to the leaves.
- If you feel that your plants could do with a pick-me-up, add a tablespoon of Chemicult and/or a tablespoon of Seagro or Kelpak. In a separate container, mix these with the necessary liquid, then strain it before filling the sprayer.

COMMON PLANT DISEASES

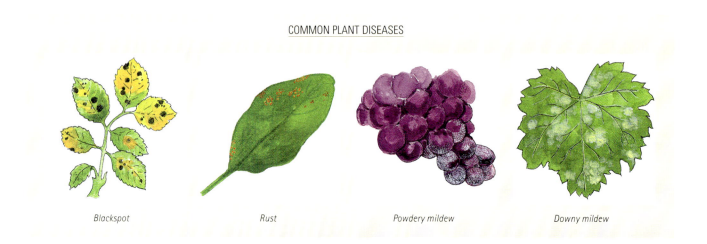

Blackspot   Rust   Powdery mildew   Downy mildew

Yet others, such as SCALE, APHIDS and TWIG WILTERS, suck the very sap out of stems. They are the survivors and deserve our admiration as well as our dislike. Once again, there are death-dealing chemicals for each of these. Such harsh remedies are useful if there is a real infestation, but many of these pests can be picked off at their first appearance, before they start breeding.

ROSE BEETLES and other BEETLES will head straight for yellow roses, but will be equally attracted to a bucket or tin painted yellow and partly filled with insecticide and a little honey or sugar.

STEM BORER will make itself known by the wilting stems of its host. Cut back carefully until you find the culprit and destroy it.

RED SPIDER MITE creep up on us while we're not looking, spreading their webs on the underside of leaves and sucking the goodness out of them. Pick off any affected leaves and destroy them completely. Then keep a careful lookout for future visits. Red spider mites hate humidity, so a good spray of water under the leaves will soon deal with them.

CUTWORMS are nefarious little creatures, creeping up on succulent seedlings and plants, and nipping them off at the base. They like to stay close to their source of food. Dig lightly into the soil and you will usually find them in a crescent close to the ailing plants. Otherwise, if you have the patience, put a collar of paper or cardboard around each newly planted seedling. They will not bother to climb over this.

Fruit is constantly under attack by FLIES, WASPS and CATERPILLARS. The codling moth is probably the worst culprit, and, as always, prevention is vastly better than cure. Make sure that you wait for the proper time period to elapse between spraying and eating the fruit and vegetables.

Try hanging tins of insecticide, honey and pounded dried peaches or apricots among fruit trees, slanting the tin to keep out the rain. Insects will not be able to resist this absolute feast. To prevent insect pests from climbing up the trunks of fruit trees, bind sticky paper around the trunk, or even strips of corrugated paper, under which insects will lurk and be easily caught.

SNAILS like to cling to the damp, shady side of flowerpots, under stones and in the heart of strap-leafed plants. Search for them there. Snails and slugs both love beer, so place a saucer of beer on the ground and hopefully they will drown in their delight. Neither creature can move on surfaces such as crushed eggshells or soot, so sprinkle these around your plants. Conversely a good, slippery layer of Vaseline around the rim of ceramic pots will keep them out of the plants within.

Though MOLES cause devastation, it seems that no effective remedy has been found. Attractive plants such as bulbs can be placed in wire or plastic mesh

COMMON INSECT PESTS

Scale

Aphids

Stink bug

CMR beetle

Cutworm

Whitefly

baskets or even into cardboard cartons. The latter will eventually disintegrate and can be removed when the bulbs are lifted.

LAWN PESTS

Crickets can make unsightly and damaging holes. Bring them to the surface by pouring soapy water down the holes.

Lawn caterpillars can devastate lawns in mid-summer, chewing up all green growth. Check by soaking the dry, yellow patches of lawn with soapy water - or leaving a wet sack on the lawn overnight. Both methods will cause the caterpillars to emerge. Apply

Lawn caterpillar

Dipterex or Karbaspray to areas infected by caterpillars and other insect pests, or cover the area with organic tobacco dust.

CREATURE COMFORT

While there is a large number of insects which chew away at our plants, there are also many insects and other creatures which do no harm at all but actually prey on the plant-feasters. Get to know these and vow to make them welcome in your garden.

Toads and frogs feed on flying ants and other insects. A ladybird will obligingly gobble up aphids and scale. Assassin bugs dine on caterpillars. That black and yellow beetle scuttling on the ground is a tiger beetle in search of other insects to eat. It is not the CMR beetle it slightly resembles. Chameleons and lizards are always on the look-out for an insect meal. Spiders, weaving webs of unbelievable intricacy, also catch insects you might regard as pests.

WEEDS

It is said that a good crop of weeds means a well-nourished garden. But no gardener will let them stay,

RIGHT *Pretty and pink – healthy roses and fuchsias with a border of thriving* Begonia semperflorens. *These plants all count among the favourites of a variety of pests. Keeping them in vigorous good health is your first line of defence.*

as they take up nourishment meant for garden plants. They can also harbour diseases and insects.

Always remove weeds before they set seed, otherwise you will have thousands of new weeds and years of tiresome labour. If you are in a hurry, pull off the weeds' flowerheads. Newly emerged weeds can be gently hoed out or even cut down with scissors. If there are no seeds on the removed weeds, chop them up and place them on the compost heap or put them into a tub of water.

After a week or two use this as a liquid fertilizer for watering or spraying onto plants. Mulching and close-planting are also effective methods of weed control. A healthy, vigorously growing lawn for example, crowds out weeds.

In summer a particularly weedy patch of ground can be covered with plastic sheeting, well fastened down at the edges. The weeds will be slowly broiled and smothered.

Herbicides

There are three major kinds of herbicide: contact, best for annual weeds; residual, which stays in the soil for some time and is taken up by the roots; and systemic, which is best for perennial weeds.

Broadleaf herbicides destroy only those with broad leaves, the dicotyledons. Others deal with grasses and allied plants and here the greatest care should be taken, for just one contact can kill a plant you certainly meant to protect.

Herbicides are particularly useful for destroying weeds growing between paving stones. In fact, it is a good idea to apply herbicide to the soil before laying the paving.

Weeds in the lawn

A weed-free lawn is a joy to behold, so tackle them steadily and you will eventually have a lawn which is strong enough to withstand any new onslaught. The best way to combat weeds is to cultivate and maintain a strong-growing, thick spread of lawn with no gaps. Mow often, rather than mowing irregularly and then cutting off too much at once.

Keep up a programme of regular feeding and watering and your close-growing, vigorous lawn will crowd out weeds.

NATURAL WAYS TO COMBAT PESTS AND DISEASES

- The first line of defence against most insects is to disturb them. When watering plants, wash off the leaves to force insects to leave their camouflaged, safe environment – they will soon fall prey to a host of predators.
- Buy a cheap laundry basket for collecting weeds and rubbish as you work.
- Never allow weeds to seed. As they flower, snip these off.
- Plant marigolds very close together, and when they have flowered but not yet seeded, cut them up and dig them into the soil. This should help to combat eelworms.
- To make your own spray base, grate 50 g Sunlight or blue mottled soap and dissolve in 500 ml boiling water. When dissolved, make this up to 5 litres with cold water.
- Make a garlic spray for use on aphids: mix the squeezed juice of 125 g garlic in 500 ml water and add to the soap solution.
- For onion spray, mix the juice of 500 g chopped onion with the soap solution. Use at half strength for mites and aphids.
- Chop the leaves of unwanted tomato plants. Boil a good handful and a few stems in a litre of water. Strain and add to the soap solution. Use to combat aphids and scale.
- For a khakibos spray useful for aphids and scale, take two handfuls of leaves, soak them in a litre of water overnight, then strain and add to the soap solution.
- For a nicotine spray boil 50 g tobacco in 4,5 litres water. Strain and add to the soap solution. Use one part to four parts water to spray mites, aphids, thrips and white fly.
- Skimmed milk has been found to be highly effective against mosaic virus in tomato plants.
- On a damp, overcast day, go out into the garden and search your agapanthus, day lilies, phormiums and other strap-leaved plants, where you will surely find snails.
- Garlic and pelargoniums planted near roses will keep aphids and beetles away.
- Insects hate herbs such as fennel, thyme, rosemary, lavender, artemesia and wormwood, all of which can be dissolved in water, strained and used as a spray.
- Add 10 drops of essential oil of lavender to 5 litres of water and use this as a spray to keep insects away.

Index

Published by Metz Press 2002
Unit 106, Hoheizen Park 1, Hoheizen Avenue,
Hoheizen 7530 South Africa

Copyright © Metz Press 2002
Text copyright © Nancy Gardiner
Photographs © Nancy Gardiner
Illustrations © Metz Press
Source for map on page 28: *Wonderful Waterwise Gardening*
(Tafelberg 2000) by Ernst van Jaarsveld.

PUBLISHER	Wilsia Metz
EDITOR	Sandra Sharpe
CONSULTANT	Sandy Munro
COVER & BOOK DESIGN	Lindie Metz, jack
ILLUSTRATIONS	Nicky Miles
INDEX	Nikki Metz
PRODUCTION	Ilse Volschenk & Andrew de Kock
REPRODUCTION	Cape Imaging Bureau, Cape Town
PRINTING AND BINDING	Tien Wah Press, Singapore
ISBN	1-875001-67-0